Discovering David's Destiny

Insightful expositions to help Christians discover their personal destiny

by Timothy J. Winters D. Min.

MOUNT CARMEL BOOKS

Also by Dr. Timothy Winters

OVERCOMING MEDIOCRITY
A DOSE OF DOCTRINE

Printed in the United States of America

ISBN 1-930899-21-1

DESIGN BY JEFF STANTON

Published by Mount Carmel Books, a subsidiary of Brazos Currents Worldwide

This book is gratefully dedicated to
the loving memory of my parents,
Albert and Louise Winters

TABLE OF CONTENTS

Foreword

I have detected across the chasm of the years that the one central aim of the expository and exegetical gifts of Dr. Timothy Winters is to let the Scriptures tell its own exalted, edifying and eternal message.

With all my years of serious Bible study, through the exegesis, exposition, and illumination of Dr. Winters, I still found a refreshing illumination and a clearer, deeper and greater understanding of this familiar Old Testament character. Dr. Winters' God-given gifts of scriptural analysis and synthesis have made him not only a household name in the Christian community but also one of the most widely sought-after Bible expositors in the country today.

Those who have a hunger for the bread and a thirst for the water of life will have their hunger satisfied and their thirst quenched by the exposition of this stimulating publication.

I commend and recommend this book to all believers without reservation.

A. Louis Patterson, Jr., Pastor
Mount Corinth Baptist Church
Houston, Texas

Introduction

As a boy, when I first heard my father tell the story of how David slew Goliath with a slingshot, he immediately became one of my favorite Bible characters. My admiration for David has burned as low flames in my heart since that night. However, those flames burst into a full blaze of appreciation as the Holy Spirit led me through the weekly preparations of the messages that now comprise the chapters of this book.

The detailed analysis of David's life strengthened the Bayview congregation and me. It was also a time for learning more about the grace, mercy and providence of God. The sovereignty of God is seen in the choice of David to be the King of Israel while he was a lowly shepherd boy. The protection of God is seen in the riveting accounts of his near escapes while running from Saul. And the provision of God is seen when David ultimately became king. David's Godly qualities emerge in every circumstance, condition and situation he faced; including his failures and sins.

Discovering David's Destiny through the pages of the inspired Word of God brought fresh insights from the reservoir of this old story. Every experience of his life is a curriculum in itself. My prayer is that the readers of this book will be edified and find comparisons of their destiny to David's destiny.

A MAN AFTER GOD'S OWN HEART

Chapter One

1 Samuel 13:14

The life of David consumes the largest portion of the Old Testament. As a matter of fact, other than Jesus Christ, no biblical character has more chapters than David. It is estimated that there are also approximately fifty-nine references to David in the New Testament. This is more than any other Old Testament character. So, based on the strength of the voluminous appearances of David in the Bible, it suggests that we should give attentive consideration to his life as it is presented in scripture by the inspiration of the Holy Spirit.

My intention with this book is to stimulate our imagination with inspiration about our own destiny. The fact is that God desires to lead us to broader destinies than we are presently experiencing. Nothing dramatizes and demonstrates that fact more than God's call of a shepherd boy to become king of Israel! Nevertheless, for some people, the slightest consideration of broader dimensions of their destiny is not a fleeting possibility. For many people an improved life in any dimension is not a consideration at all because they lack the ability to imagine themselves above their current circumstances. This is not a reference to people who we would identify as disenfranchised. I am referring to people who could be described as productive citizens who are unknowingly caught up in *stagnation and status quo*. It is similar to the fellow who said, "I dig the ditch to make the money to buy the food to gain the strength to dig the ditch."

No doubt someone will read this book whose life is a cycle of monotony – no higher, no lower, no better, no worse. Many people, regardless of color and walk of life, have settled for the monotonous recurring routine of their existence, including Christians. However, a certain kind of person responds to inspiration for a broader destiny. David is a classic example! To transition from a shepherd to a sovereign is an indisputable illustration of deepening one's destiny. To move from *handling* a *staff* to *holding a scepter* is the epitome of following God's call to new levels in destiny. To be a keeper of sheep and to later become a *king over souls* is the pure essence of sailing into the uncharted waters of new destinies.

Since all people are not eager to go through new doors to new pathways and on to new destines, an appropriate question that can be asked is what kind of people are lifted up by the possibility of an enriched destiny? Who is it that accepts a promotion by an opportunity from God to an unusual destiny? The answer? People like David! David represents people who God can choose for a special destiny. David's destiny was affixed to the descriptive words, "a man after God's own heart." In a court of law, those words would be Exhibit #1. Furthermore, they would be the only exhibits needed to show how David's life took such an incredible turn. The total evidence to show how David became king of Israel are the words: *he was a man after God's own heart.*

David Was Sovereignly Chosen

For me, one of the most intriguing and fascinating characteristics about God is His sovereignty. God can do what He wants to do, anytime He wants to do it, with whomever He wants to. He does not have to obtain permission. Neither does He have to have an evaluation. That is known as *sovereignty!* The other side of sovereignty is no one else can do anything that God does not want them to do. God's sovereign work is always to accomplish eternal good even when we do not understand or can't appreciate it. This is true especially when something unpleasant occurs. God can make it achieve good. God's ability is not hindered to work good out of something that is wrong. Consequently, whomever God chooses to bless will be blessed and whomever God chooses to promote, will be promoted. This is promised in Psalm 1: "*He shall be like a tree planted by the rivers of waters, his leaf also shall not wither and whatsoever he does shall prosper.*"

When God takes aim, He does not miss! Then, the only appropriate conclusion is David was the sovereign choice by God to be the King of Israel.

A valid question for consideration is that if God was looking for a man after His own heart, why did He choose David? David was a sheepherder -- the least among his brethren. He was even the least in the sight of his own father. When Samuel came to Jesse's house with a word from God that the next king was one of his sons, Jesse presented Samuel with only seven of his sons. When Samuel did not receive confirmation for any of those sons, he said to Jesse, "Are these all your sons?" It was only then that Jesse remembered David, who was out in the field with the sheep. The question still remains, why did God choose David?

A look into the New Testament at the writings of the Apostle

Paul will help answer the question. Paul wrote these inspirational words to the Corinthians:

> *"…not many mighty, not many noble are called*
> *But God has chosen the foolish things of the world*
> *to confound the wise; and God has chosen the weak*
> *things of the world to confound the things which are*
> *mighty;*
> *And base things of the world, and things which are*
> *Despised, has God chosen, yes, and things which are*
> *Not, to bring to nothing things that are,*
> **So that no flesh should glory in His presence."**
> (1 Corinthians 1:26-28)

God chooses foolish things, weak things, base things and despised things *so that no flesh may glory in* **H***is presence!* God chooses those who are unworthy so He will receive the glory for whatever we accomplish. It was David who alluded to our unworthiness in Psalm 8 when he said, "*What is man that* **Y***ou are mindful of him?*" The sovereignty of God simply blew his mind. This question emerged out of his personal quandary. And what is more, he expressed his quandary again in 1 Chronicles 29:14 when he said:

> *"But who am I, and what are my people, that we should*
> *be able to offer so willingly after this sort? For all things*
> *come from you, and of your own have we given unto you."*

That statement was made in thanksgiving unto God for the abundant offering that had been received for the construction of the Temple. It was the recognition that God had first given unto them so they in turn could give back to God. It was also the recognition of God's sovereignty. The call of David to be **k**ing of Israel, like our call to salvation and service, was based on God's sovereignty.

I have been unable to locate from any source of research that David was expecting to become **k**ing of Israel. It was not on his prayer list. He did not "name and claim" to become king. The clear teaching of scripture is that God sovereignly chose him.

David's Spiritual Character

David's spiritual character is also described in the words "*a man after God's heart*." David's heart was toward God, and more than that, he had a heart like God's heart. David was a loving person and people loved him. The simple fact is with a heart like God David loved the way God loves. He possessed in human quality many of the characteristics of God. The ultimate reality about David is that he loved God with all his heart!

Another question worthy of consideration is if David loved the way God loved and had a heart like God, how then could he have gotten involved with Bathsheba and, later on, order her husband to be killed? That certainly is a valid question. The truth is, however, there was a trail of foolish decisions and dumb mistakes in David's life long before Bathsheba. The difference is the incident with Bathsheba has far more notoriety. The answer goes back to the first two words that describe his spiritual character: *a man after God's own heart*.

Lest we forget, David was A MAN! In spite of how high God lifted him, underneath he was still *a man*. Even though he was known as the sweet singer in Israel, underneath he was still *a man*. Even though he was a magnificent warrior, underneath he was still *a man*. In spite of his God-like qualities, underneath he was still a man. This is not mentioned to excuse David's weaknesses, but rather to *express* them. Yes, to admit them. As a man, he possessed all the human flaws and frailties of any other mortal being. Nevertheless, the same incident that accusers would use to expose him also *exonerates* him. He did what was wrong because he was **a man**, but then he did what was right because he was **a man after God's own heart!**

There are people, including Christians, who will not say, "I am sorry," even when they are proven wrong. Neither will they say, "Please forgive me." David's heart-wrenching confession is recorded in Psalm 51: "*Have mercy upon me O God, according to your loving kindness. Create in me a clean heart.*"

Those are the words of a man who has a heart like God!

David *stumbled* because he was *a man*, but he *survived* because he was a man *after God's own heart*. There should not be any strong animosity on our part toward David. If we want God to "get" David, He would have to "get" us also. After all, the same grace that was bestowed upon David is the same grace that has been bestowed upon us. We were called by the same standard by which David was called-- by God's sovereignty and grace.

David's Strong Contribution

We would all agree that David's service to the Lord could be described as a strong contribution. It was not a hit and miss or on and off contribution, but a strong contribution. His life shows us that a person can lose a battle and still win the war. David shows all who have fallen that they don't have to stay down. There are few Christians who don't know the 23rd Psalm. Most Christians can recite some or portions of David's Psalms. We sing his Psalms, and I even pray his prayers.

Consider this scenario. What if God had fired David for his sin? If David had been fired, we would not have his Psalms that bless our souls in times of despair. We would not have his encouraging words: "*Fret not thyself because of evil doers, and neither be thou envious of the workers of iniquity, they shall soon be cut down like the grass.*" We would not have another favorite Psalm that reads: "*The Lord is my light and my salvation, whom shall I fear? The Lord is the strength of my life, of whom shall I be afraid.*"

If God had fired David we would not have his admonishment to, "*Wait on the Lord and be of good courage.*" There is history behind those words. There is personal experience with God behind the inspiration of those words. If God had fired David, He would have had to change the whole order of prophecy concerning Jesus Christ, the son of David. The record is that Jesus will sit on the throne of His father, David, forever. And of His kingdom there shall be no end!

In the following chapters we will not only learn a lot about King David but we will also learn a lot about God. We will see how long-suffering God can really be, how deeply God can love, and the extent that God can forgive and restore. All of that will come to the surface as we study the life of this remarkable man of God. We should want to deepen our relationship with God who can forgive and restore the way David was forgiven and restored. We should want to strengthen our fellowship with God who was so long suffering with David.

For the person who does not know God, you should want to know the God who can reach down and dust off a shepherd boy and bring him all the way to the throne of Israel! Some of us may know what it's like when forgiveness has been withheld from us by others or to be written off by others. However, the record of David's life shows that God can write you back in. We see the awesomeness of God as David's life intersects with his destiny.

GOD'S CHOICE

Chapter Two

1 Samuel 16:1-13

Without a doubt there are people all over the world who have paid the high price of not making God's choice their choice. Consequently, we all know the difference between what our choices have turned out to be in comparison to what God's choices for us would have been. We can but speculate about how different our lives would be if we had paid attention to God's choice. We have learned the hard way that God's choice for us is always the best – learned in the "school of experience" that when God points us in a direction it is the best direction for us to take. We learned through much needless pain that when God has a plan for our lives it is the best plan. Some of us would have to admit that the most grievous mistake we've ever had was not to take the mate who was God's choice for us. Someone didn't take the wife who was God's choice. Someone else didn't take the husband who was God's choice. When we look at all the choices we have made that were contradictory to God's choice it seems like it takes a lifetime for us to learn to put our trust in God. We are slow to learn that God desires the best for us.

Therefore, when we contrast Israel's choice for a king with God's choice, we will see a glaring difference. And, the same can be said about our own choices when we compare them to God's choices for us. I confess that every choice I have made that was not God's choice has ended up in disaster.

I'm in the group who learned the hard way that God's choice is *always right* and God's choice is *always best.* David is a classic example. To be called from herding sheep and eventually crowned king of a nation is undeniable proof of the best choices God has for His own.

The life of David shows us that God is looking for people who He can promote to higher levels of service. Conversely, there are people who God will *not* promote. The qualities that a person must have to be chosen of God, used of God, and promoted by God are primarily spiritual qualities. The Lord says, "*Seek ye first the kingdom of heaven and all these things will be added unto you.*" The apostle Paul admonishes us by saying, "*Set your affections on things that are above and not on things here below.*" In other words, we must put God first. We must make God our top priority. That is the main quality God is looking for. We have already seen that David's heart was turned toward God.

The Command to Samuel

At the time of the text, Samuel performed three clerical responsibilities to the nation of Israel. He had triple roles of leadership for the people of God. He was a prophet, priest and judge. Actually, he was the last authentic judge in Israel. Lest we forget, God spoke to His people then as he does now *through the man of God.* And the total weight of the narrative rests on the closing sentence of verse one where the Lord says, "*I have provided me a king among his (Jesse's) sons.*" So he gave the command to Samuel:

"Go fill your horn with oil and start in the direction of Jesse's house. The next king is among his sons."

I don't want you to forget this: whenever God commands us to do something, He has already made the provision for us to do it. Every time.

The occasion when the disciples fished all night and caught nothing is an example. Luke gives the story in the fifth chapter. While they were washing out their nets in dejection and frustration, the Lord commanded them to launch out into the deep for a "catch." He apparently had made the provision while Peter was protesting His command. "*Master we have toiled all night and have caught nothing.*"

I imagine that a large school of fish was just swimming around in circles waiting for them to go out there and drop the net down over them. However, the problem was getting the disciples to understand that the provision had already been made. In response to Peter's leadership they finally went back out to sea and dropped their net and they "*enclosed a great multitude of fish.*"

Our problem today is following God's command to get where the provision is. It was Samuel's problem also. Samuel represents the sluggish and slow steps that we take in response to a command from God. Nevertheless, Samuel cautiously made his way to Jesse's house.

Hindsight shows us where Saul had led Israel was no comparison to where David would lead them. Yet Samuel was mourning for Saul. God eventually told him, "*Stop mourning for Saul. Fill your horn with oil. Get ready to anoint the next king of Israel. Saul is not going to be king much longer.*" What was actually going on in this narrative was that *God was making a personnel change.* God does that on occasion, you know. In corporate America it is not uncommon. In the sports world there are many former head coaches who are looking for a job. They were removed because a personnel change was necessary.

God also makes personnel changes. Saul was not the only king that God removed. God removed a king named Belshazzar with a mysterious inscription written on the king's wall. And, before that God displaced Belshazzar's grandfather, Nebuchadnezzar, in even more dramatic fashion.

Personnel changes are a manager's nightmare and a pastor's nightmare as well. Personnel changes are particularly difficult in the church because we forget that God's *plan and purpose has priority over any person.* We tend to become nostalgic over people we have served with for a while and when our favorite person moves on, or is moved on, we act as Samuel did when it was time to remove Saul. An invaluable lesson that church people need to learn is that no one is indispensable. God was doing all right before any of us got here and He may be better off when some of us are gone.

You may notice from verse two the excuses that Samuel made and the hesitancy of his response. His response to God was, "*Lord, if I go to Jesse's house Saul will kill me.*" I sure hope you see the irony in Samuel's objection. The man he was mourning about would kill him if he knew what he was going to Jesse's house to do. It's almost humorous, isn't it? But, the main emotion that Samuel was struggling with was fear. Fear keeps us from following God's directions to new and better experiences. However, God summarized His command to Samuel by saying, "*I will show you what to do.*"

What reassuring words these must have been to the aging prophet. Notwithstanding, the likely possibility is that God is nudging some Christians today to new and better experiences, but they are afraid they won't hear God saying, "*I will show you what to do.*" God wants to take us to places we have never been before, and help us to function at a level we have never served at before. And all we need to do is hear Him saying, "*I will show you what to do.*" It may be a business God wants you to start, or a new ministry He wants you to lead, and your resource is having Him show you what to do.

Apparently God's promise to show Samuel what to do calmed his fears. He went to fulfill his mission. When Samuel arrived the townfolk in Bethlehem trembled and they asked whether he was coming peaceably. Their knees began knocking when the watcher announced, "*Samuel is coming.*" The irony is that they were afraid of him *coming* to Bethlehem and he had been afraid of *going* to Bethlehem. I hasten to clarify that they were afraid of him because of the power of God in his life. It means we can walk more confidently in response to God's directions for our lives than we tend to do.

The Consideration of the Sons

Even though Samuel had God's promise that the next king was among the sons of Jesse it was still necessary for him to give all of Jesse's sons consideration in the selection. Therefore, all seven of Jesse's sons paraded before him for personal inspection and the hint is that he liked all of them. He was impressed with all of them. All of them passed Samuel's test to be the next king, especially the oldest son. His name was Eliab, and when he stood before the prophet, Samuel may have thought, "*This is going to be an easy assignment. I can be on my way back home in a few minutes.*"

But, this marks the difference between our choice and *God's* choice. We are often impressed by *external qualities*, but God is impressed by *internal qualities.* We are impressed by *physical appearance*, whereas God is impressed with *spiritual aptitude.* The difference between the two is hardly similar. Samuel was certain the first son was the next king. He said to himself, "*Surely the LORD'S anointed is before Him.*"

I imagine that's when he took the cork out of his horn and turned it upside down to pour the oil and anoint Eliab the next king of Israel, but no oil flowed. It coagulated. And six other times the same thing happened. God then chastised Samuel with these words: "*Look not on his countenance or on the height of his stature, because I have refused him; for the LORD sees not as man sees; for man looks on the outward appearance, but the LORD looks on the heart.*" Samuel learned the meaning of those words personally.

Later on in the narrative at Chapter 17, the Lord allows us to see the inner quality of Eliab. The story in Chapter 17 is about when David came to the battlefield when Goliath was making his challenge for Israel to choose a man to fight him. The story line shows that Eliab overheard David inquiring about what would be done for the person who killed the giant. Verse 28 reads: "*And Eliab, his eldest brother, heard when he spoke to the men; and Eliab's anger was kindled against David and he said, 'Why have you come down here and with whom have you left those few sheep? I know your pride and the haughtiness of your heart. You have come down that you might see the battle.'*"

Those accusative and caustic words show us a few things about Eliab's heart. First of all, they indicate he had an *angry* heart. It says he became angry when he overheard David inquiring about the reward to be given to the person who killed the giant. Anyone who has the unfortunate experience of dealing with someone who has an angry heart will have absolute pure misery to contend with. People who have angry hearts don't like anyone. Nothing pleases them. You have to tiptoe around them for fear they may explode about most anything at any minute. Anything can set them off. *Eliab had an angry heart.*

He not only had an angry heart, he also had a *suspicious heart*. People with suspicious hearts are always looking and checking for hidden meaning in anything anyone says or does. They are always looking for a *smoking gun*. They don't accept anything at face value. *Eliab had a suspicious heart.*

Nevertheless, he didn't only have an *angry heart* and *suspicious heart*, but he also had a *cynical heart*. He said to David, "*Who have you left those few sheep with*?" There is a good chance, however, that Jesse had more than a few sheep. The strong possibility is that Jesse was the owner of a whole bunch of sheep. But, the intent of referring to them as a few sheep was to demean David. In teen vernacular, it was to "put David down."

And, he asserted that he knew David's pride. Now isn't that something to say about the person the Bible says was "*a man after God's own heart*?" He told David, "*I know the haughtiness of your heart.*"

Eliab was really revealing the content of his own heart. That's really what was happening. In essence Eliab didn't have enough perception to see the spiritual qualities in his own brother, who was raised up in the same household with him. One of the main qualities of a king was to have perception. A king would have to be a good judge of character. And, if he couldn't properly judge the character of his own brother, how was he going to judge the character of strangers who would come before him? God knew this, but Samuel didn't.

So, God refused Eliab.

The next son was Abinadab, and Samuel heard God say, "*Neither has the LORD chosen this one.*"

And, the next son was Shammah, and again God told Samuel, "*Neither has the LORD chosen this one.*"

The final word from Samuel to Jesse, after seven consecutive sons had passed before him, was: "*The LORD has not chosen these.*"

Samuel must have been in the throes of a frustrating quandary like many Christians who have followed God's instructions with no results. But, in that case we should await more instructions. That's what Samuel did. He asked Jesse, "*Are these all the sons that you have?*"

Jesse apparently finally remembered that he had another son named David. So he responded and said, "*There remains yet the youngest, and behold he keeps the sheep.*"

That is a very revealing statement. It means that not only was David disdained by his brethren, he was disdained by his father as well. That may have been David's inspiration to take up his pen to write Psalm 27:10: "*When my father and mother forsake me, then the Lord will take me up.*"

The content of Jesse's statement is disturbingly enlightening. However, the meaning is obscured by the poetic 16th century English translation. He said, "*there remains the youngest.*" The Hebrew word that is translated "remains" is *qatan*. It means **little**, **least** or **young**. But, it also carries the meaning of **insignificant** or **unimportant**. And, that is the meaning we must take for clarification of the remainder of the statement.

He continued to say, "*Behold, he keeps the sheep.*" Take note of the "behold." We hardly use that word and when we do use it we are probably reading it in the Bible. The word, "behold" is intended to be instructional. It means, "look." He actually meant, "*Look, he keeps sheep.*"

That refers to the insignificance of the employment of a shepherd. Notice he didn't' even say who the shepherd boy was. He never called David's name. Everyone in that culture knew a shepherd was at the bottom rung of the employment ladder in Israel. But, that didn't deter Samuel at all. He told Jesse to "*Send and get him; we will not sit down (to eat) till he comes here.*" Samuel threatened that no one would be permitted to take a single sip of wine until David arrived, and that not one crust of bread would be tasted until David got there.

The Choice of the Sovereign

The Sovereign, of course, refers to God. David was the choice of the Sovereign.

David's arrival was accompanied by the only physical description that is given of him. Once again, we must be careful to watch that old King James English or the meaning will be lost. He is described as being *ruddy*. From the Hebrew that means "dark, reddened complexion." Most of the commentaries I have read on David say he had red hair. However, the description isn't that he had red hair, but that he was of reddened complexion.

The description also indicates he had good *countenance*. That is an internal description. Countenance emanates from the inside and is reflected on the outside. There are a whole lot of good-looking people who do not have good countenance.

Then it also says he was *handsome* and the terminology of our day would call him a good-looking dude. Nevertheless, David was not God's choice because of his looks, but because of his love – not because he was *handsome*, but because of his *heart*. However, we shouldn't miss the fact that all of Jesse's sons were good-looking men. The hint of the narrative is that Samuel was impressed with all of them and tried to pour the oil out on all of them.

They were all good-looking, which suggests to us that that God's choice of David had to be more than his good looks. God's choice of David was based on his inner qualities not his outer qualities. With the confirming words of God to "*arise and anoint him*" Samuel again uncorked the horn and it poured like a Texas oil well.

This must have been the occasion that David reflected upon to write Psalm 23:5, *He anoints my head with oil, my cup runs over*, and he mentioned *it was in the presence of my enemies.* In the same space that describes the anointing it says, "*The Spirit of the LORD came upon him from that day onward.*"

That was mentioned because the position of king over Israel was, first and foremost, a spiritual position, which was not the case with the other neighboring king. David needed spiritual resources to be king over God's people. So it says, "*The spirit of the Lord came up on him.*"

In Old Testament times the Holy Spirit ministered externally by coming upon a person. The Holy Spirit would do his work and then would leave. However, the distinction with David is that it appears the Holy Spirit never left him. It says the Holy Spirit came upon him from that day onward.

During the church age the Holy Spirit indwells believers. His ministry is internal. It is significant to observe that David was blessed by ministry of Holy Spirit the same as New Testament believers. The episode of David's anointing as king of Israel closes by saying, "*So Samuel rose up and went to Ramah.*" However, the deeper implication is that he went into retirement.

The narrative does not specifically indicate what became of David after his anointing. When I have opportunity, I enjoy the television documentaries that answer the question, Whatever Happened To So and So? I enjoyed an intriguing evening some time ago watching a documentary on "Whatever Happened to the Nine Children who Integrated Central High in Little Rock, Arkansas." The integration of Central High was a major news item for several weeks during the mid '50s. The documentary showed where they all were and what they were doing. It was good to see that they all were leading productive lives.

Well, the question for our consideration is "what happened to David after his anointing?" We need to look forward to 1 Samuel Chapter 17 for the answer. This was during the time when David had become Saul's musician and armor bearer. It indicates that David wasn't given a life sentence as Saul's musician and armor bearer. He apparently was released from time to time to return home to his family. And, according to 1 Samuel 17:15, when David had opportunity to go home, "*he returned to feed his father's sheep*."

There again is one of David's spiritual qualities that rose to the surface. How likely would it be if anyone else who had been anointed to be the next king of Israel would return home and herd sheep? Very unlikely, I suspect. That speaks volumes about David's inner spiritual qualities.

The application for this story is that we don't have to be pushy or impatient about anything that God has promised to provide for us. There is absolutely no reason to scheme, connive, undercut or backstab anyone for what the Lord has promised us.

We will see later that David had several opportunities to take the throne by force. In fact, he even stopped his own men when they had opportunities to do it for him. He had as many opportunities to kill Saul as Saul made attempts to kill him. Whatever the Lord has promised us, He can and will deliver it.

David modeled his own words. They could have been written against the backdrop of him herding sheep after he was declared to be the next king of Israel. This could have been the foundation for Psalm 27:14 where he urges the people of God to, "*Wait on the Lord*." We don't have to hasten the delivery of the blessing but simply wait on the Lord. And, while we are waiting we can "*be of good courage*." While you are waiting, "*the Lord will strengthen your heart*." Then he said again, "*wait I say, on the Lord*."

David is encouraging us to continue to do what we've already been doing while we are waiting. We should keep on serving the way we've always served while waiting on the Lord. That's what David did. He went back to herding sheep even though he had been anointed and pronounced to be the next king of Israel. That's remarkable behavior and we should strive diligently to emulate it.

A ROYAL INVITATION

Chapter Three

I Samuel 16: 14-23

God uses the circumstances of our lives and the circumstances of other people for our personal development. Our circumstances and situations become the unwritten chapters of our lives and our lives change by the movement of people into and out of our lives. We change by our own promotion, or demotion, and by the promotion, or demotion, of people who are in our immediate circle of socialization.

This was precisely the case with David and Saul. When Samuel gave the prophetic pronouncement that God was going to rend the kingdom from Saul, the pronouncement affected all of Israel. But, it affected no one the way it affected David. Saul's movement *from* the throne was David's movement to the throne.

Nevertheless, it must be stated clearly that it was never in

David's mind that he would replace Saul while Saul was still king! Consequently, he never made a move to dethrone Saul. He never lifted one finger to displace him. Furthermore, the narrative will reveal later that David had several opportunities to kill Saul. On one occasion his men urged him to seize the moment, thinking that fate had provided him the opportunity to kill Saul, but he didn't do it and wouldn't permit them to do it either!

The text opens with a dreadful description of Saul. The Spirit of the Lord had departed from Saul and an evil spirit had come and troubled him. An emotional disquietness beset him. What the modern diagnosis of his ailment would be is impossible for us to discern. But I suggest that whatever his illness was, it was as much *spiritual* as it was *emotional* and was as much *spiritual* as it was *mental.* We should know that the three conditions interconnect; spiritual, emotional and mental components connect one to the other. We are not completely whole until all three components are connected and are mutually working. Isaiah 26:3 put it succinctly: "*God will keep your heart in perfect peace when your mind is stayed on Him.*"

Many a song has come out of the Black church experience that underscores the connection between the spiritual, emotional and mental dimensions of our existence. Lyrics of an old song are, "*I woke up this morning with my mind stayed on Jesus.*" And, lyrics of another are, "*Keep my heart, keep my hands, keep my soul I pray.*"

Those songs were composed and sung in recognition of the harmonious connection that should exist between our spiritual, emotional and mental components. Unfortunately, for Saul this was not the case. Saul was stricken with an acute complex mental disorder.

When we read of Saul's life, we will see that he grew more and more distant from God until he reached the point where he was completely independent of God. But, as we read the story of Saul's life we will see that he always had a tendency to act independently of God.

Saul did not have the personal, intimate relationship with God that David did. As a matter of fact, *there are no recorded prayers of King Saul.* There is no record where he ever admonished his people to turn to God. Furthermore, there is no record where Saul ever personally prayed! Saul reached the point where he acted independently. And, the extent of his independence was the day when he took it upon himself to stand where only the man of God should stand! He performed an act that only the man of God should perform.

In Jewish religious practice, when there was a great victory a sacrifice would be offered to give thanks unto God. There was the occasion when Saul had led his army to a great victory. However, he did not think Samuel was going to arrive in time to offer the sacrifice, so he offered it himself. Saul, because of his distance and independence from God did not, perhaps, realize the seriousness of his offense.

Understand, please, that being king did not make him qualified to stand where only the man of God should stand. God jealously guards that place Himself. Samuel did eventually arrive and discovered what Saul had done. That is when Samuel announced to Saul that God would take the kingdom from him.

There is a theological point that I want to highlight before going any further. We should not attempt to draw theological conclusions about the ministry of the Holy Spirit from this text. It says, explicitly, "*the Spirit of the LORD departed from Saul.*"

Regrettably, people who claim that a person can lose his or her salvation use Saul to make their point. In particular they refer to this scripture that shows the Spirit of the LORD left him and an evil spirit came to trouble him. We must keep in mind the function of the Holy Spirit was different in Old Testament times than in New Testament times. In the Old Testament He came upon a person for empowerment, direction, deliverance, or for some specific other reason. In the Old Testament the ministry of the Holy Spirit was *external* and always *temporary*. In those times it was not unusual for the Holy Spirit to leave a person!

However, in the New Testament His ministry is *internal* and *permanent*. The exception, however, is David! Note the end of verse 13, which says, "*The Spirit of the LORD came upon him from that day onward.*" The Holy Spirit never left David!

But, in the New Testament we refer specifically to the words of our Lord in John 14:16: "*And I will pray to the Father, and he shall give you another Comforter, that He may abide with you forever.*" Thus, the theological emphasis that a person can lose salvation based on Saul's experience of the Holy Spirit leaving him is grossly erroneous.

Nonetheless, the mental condition of Saul was the background for David to receive a royal invitation!

It Was A Delightful Invitation

Make no mistake about it: for a teenage shepherd boy to receive a personal invitation from the King would certainly be delightful. For example, if I received an invitation from the White House, I do not know what could keep me from going to meet the President of the United States. It would not matter if he were a Democrat or a Republican. In either case, it would be a delightful invitation. What's more, David's invitation was delightful in the way it originated. It came at the suggestion of some of Saul's servants. The servants were concerned about Saul's dreadful mental state and they wanted to acquire some measure of relief for his disturbed psyche. So the conclusion was good music. The thinking was that music would somehow provide a calming affect on his mental state. That was the first consideration.

The second consideration was the person would have to be the best musician in all Israel! The person for the job really needed to know how to play. That standard as the qualification is why the person had to be the best in Israel. As a matter of fact, that qualification *excluded* a lot of musicians in Israel, but it *included* David. It *disqualified* a lot of musicians, but it *qualified* David. He was the best in Israel.

The third consideration was how to find someone that good.

They knew what they needed, but who could meet the qualifications? David was identified as the musician who was needed. In essence, one of Saul's servants said, "I know just the guy. I have heard him. This is not hearsay. Actually, he lives right down the road in Bethlehem. He is almost in earshot of us." Not only had this servant of Saul seen David he had heard him play. I will say repeatedly throughout this book that the opportunity for a broader dimension of our destiny will not matter at all if you are not prepared for the opportunity. David was prepared for his opportunity to play for the King. There is a vast difference between preparing for an opportunity and to have already prepared for an opportunity.

Verse 18 contains some of David's qualifications, but not all of them. One verse would not hold all of David's qualifications. First of all the qualifications indicate that he was *skillful*. That is to say that he played skillfully. No doubt, he used the long lazy hours of those dull days when he was shepherding his father's sheep for his rehearsal time.

I heard recently that Liberace practiced three hours every day! Even when he was on vacation he managed to include the mandatory three hours of rehearsal time. That's how he became such a great pianist. First of all, David was skillful. And secondly, he was *mighty*. That meant in addition to being skillful he was also strong. Of course that would mean physically strong, but besides being physically strong it could also mean constitutionally strong. A person must have a strong constitution in order take advantage of the opportunity for a greater destiny. You must be able to pick yourself up when you have fallen down. You must have inner strength to keep yourself going amidst the most difficult times.

Next it says he was *valiant and a man of war*. In other words, he was a strong soldier, indicating that he was a fighter, but not a fighter like someone who goes around punching people in the eye.

Every church has obstinate fighters in the congregation.

Whatever pastoral leadership offers, they are against it. It does not matter what it is. I am not talking about that kind of fighting. I am talking about a fighting spirit. When you have been knocked down, you get back up again. If you have been knocked out, you still make a comeback.

Here are David's qualities thus far: skillful, strong and a soldier. Then it says, and *prudent in matters*. This means that David was also smart. Being smart never hinders anyone. It has a way of helping you out no matter where you are or what you are doing. David was smart. Four times in chapter 18, it states that David behaved himself wisely before Saul. The meaning is that he said what he should say and did not say what he was not supposed to say. He always did what he was supposed to do. He behaved himself wisely. He was smart. He was prudent in matters. This is critical because Saul's servants didn't want someone who might see the King do something dumb in his craziness and then go out and talk about it. Therefore, David met all the criteria for his confidential assignment.

So, David was skillful, strong, a soldier, and smart, but that is not all. Another quality is listed. David was an agreeable person. Agreeable translates to *sociable*! One of the problems with people who have great skills and are really gifted is that they cannot work with anyone. They forget that their feet are touching the ground like every one else's. Consequently, it is significant that David was also sociable, meaning that he got along well with other people.

But that's still not all: he was skillful, strong, a soldier, smart, sociable "*and the Lord was with him*" which means he was *spiritual.* Whenever I interview a musician, or any staff person for that matter, spiritual quality is what I look for. It's number one! It does not matter how well a person can play an instrument, he or she must have a personal relationship with the Lord! Added to all the qualities that he possessed, David also was a spiritual man.

Now, the qualities that are highlighted from verse 18 are still not all the qualities that David possessed. Please note that these qualities first appear on the *preparation side* for service before they are visible on the performance side. This reminds me of an old Zenith appliance commercial that said, "The quality must go in before the name goes on." David was more than qualified to serve as the King's musician.

However, before leaving this point, I feel urged to say that there is someone somewhere who sees and knows and appreciates your good qualities. This verse contains a personal blessing for me to the extent that I don't intend ever to have another day when I don't feel appreciated!

All of us have had those days when we do not feel appreciated. I have had them and so have you. The days when we think, "nobody appreciates what I am doing," or days when we feel, "no one knows what I am going through." And we throw a pity party and invite a whole bunch of pitiful people to come and party with us. We have all done it. We have all felt that way.

But I can say, "No more!" I am not going to have another day when I don't feel appreciated, not after reading verse 18! After reading this verse I know there is someone, somewhere, who sees and knows and appreciates me and does not mind speaking up about it. For every person who is "dogging you out" behind your back, there is someone who is saying good things about you. You may not know it, and you may not always hear it, but someone sees and knows and appreciates who you are and what you are doing. Just as Saul's servant who spoke well of David, someone is saying good things about you and about me. Praise God!

It Was A Dangerous Invitation

Dangerous? "How so," you ask? To go from private service to public service is dangerous. Prior to this royal invitation all of David's service was mostly private between him and God. No one saw David take out that lion the other day. That lion made a mistake and came into the wrong sheepfold. Perhaps it had been going in and out of other shepherds' sheepfolds, but it made a mistake when it picked David's sheepfold. David took him out!

However, no one saw that but God.

A bear also made the same mistake and picked David's sheepfold to look for dinner. When David related the story to Saul, he said the bear had a lamb in its arms and he caught the bear by the beard and slew it. But no one saw him do that but the Lord. Most of his service up to this point had been private.

Similar danger exists in Christian service. You have not known trouble and heartache until you come out publicly to serve the Lord! It is dangerous! But the danger is no reason not to serve.

Some people try to avoid the danger of Christian service by only attending worship and not committing to a ministry. That is not an appropriate option! The danger is no reason not to serve. After all, we have the Lord's promise that He will be with us always. Many times people do not respond to the offer of enriched destiny because of the danger they see. It is easy to see more *risk* than *reward*. We often see more *opposition* than *opportunity*. We cannot see the *promotion* because we are looking at the *problem*.

The question is, what was David's danger? That's a good question. The answer is Saul! Saul was the danger! How would you like to work for a crazy person? Someone may say, "I do!" But, in honesty there is no comparison. Scripture shows that Saul went in and out of a paroxysm of jealousy toward David. Talk about a love-hate relationship, this was it!

Verse 21 indicates that Saul loved David. In fact, it says he loved David "*Greatly*!" David was the kind of guy that you had to force yourself not to love. Whoever did not love David had to work a long time at not loving him. His character attracted people to him. Even Saul loved him! But on more than one occasion, and in a fit of homicidal mania, Saul attempted to take David's life. And what's more, he pursued him like a fugitive for more than sixteen years!

So, it was a *dangerous invitation*. But the truth is, if we yield to the possibility of danger we will never leave our living rooms to go any place. If we thought about all that could go wrong, we would never get out of bed!

I have already alluded to the risks that rob us of reward, and the problems that prevent promotions. However, David shows us that danger should not be shunned. The risk is rendered negligible by the reward. Practically speaking, this was a *delightful* invitation and secondly, it was a *dangerous* invitation.

It Was A Developmental Invitation

This invitation provided David the opportunity to develop more. God used this invitation to give him exposure to the inner workings of the King's administration. And when we review our lives, we will come to the conclusion that every exposure we had, good or bad, turned out to be for our personal development. God has used every experience in our lives to stir us to where He wants us to be.

The good result of this invitation was that Saul was not crazy every day. He was not crazy all the time. So during the times when Saul was sane David had the privilege to see and learn the protocols of heads of state. He also had the opportunity to see and learn various kinds of negotiations, including foreign policy. He became acquainted with the exporting and importing of goods through foreign interchange. This helped to develop David for his future role as King. It is unrealistic to think that David would go straight from his father's sheepfold to the throne of Israel. So God orchestrated this invitation for David to work inside the King's inner circle of servants. The lessons he learned there were invaluable.

One of the problems that surfaces among some young people in our day is they want to go from the bottom straight to the top with no pause in between. However, it is essential for development to take place during the movement from the bottom to the top that will help to insure that the person will be able to stay there.

So, it was a *Delightful Invitation*, a *Dangerous Invitation* and, finally, it was a *Developmental Invitation*. It was developmental in two senses. First of all, it produced *professional* development for David and *personal* development as well. David's development is seen in the fact that he started as a musician for the King, but he didn't remain as a musician. He subsequently became Saul's s armor-bearer!

When we follow God's design for our lives, we will not only *receive exposure* but also it will *result in expansion.* When Abraham first started walking with the Lord, all he had was a promise from God about some land. And, later on God told him that He would show him the land. And, sometime after that God told him He was going to give him the land.

God also promised and gave him a son! That is the essence of allowing God to expand our destiny. The progression is clear in the story of David. He started out as a musician, but he did not stay a musician; instead, he later became Saul's armor-bearer.

The fact is that if we would not restrict ourselves so much, God would lead us on new paths to new destinies. If we didn't hinder ourselves so much, God would expand the horizons of our destinies. If we did not inhibit ourselves so much, God would use us in more enlarged capacities in His service. David's experience in development can be our experience as well. There is a good chance that God desires to promote us from where we are at the present.

There is yet another intriguing fact that is hidden beneath the surface of this narrative and, when uncovered, will reveal more spiritual qualities about David. We must understand that this invitation was not like a two-year, four-year or six-year enlistment. David did not stay in Saul's administration without a break. So the question is, what did David do when he was given personal time away from the King? Chapter, 17:15, says, "*David returned from Saul to feed his father's sheep in Bethlehem.*"

Some of us would never have looked at another sheep again after becoming the King's musician, and most certainly we wouldn't tend sheep once we were promoted to be the King's armor-bearer! However, this glimpse into David's spiritual character deepens our appreciation of him for the multiple spiritual qualities that he possessed. The quote about being "*able to walk with kings and queens and never lose the common touch*" definitely fits David. David easily made the adjustment from the King's house back to his father's house. He easily made the adjustment from the *royal palace* back the *rugged pasture*. It's a fascinating actuality that after serving on the king's personal staff David could still go back to herding sheep!

Here is the final application. David is not the only person who can boast and brag about receiving a royal invitation. As Christians we also have received a Royal Invitation. Our invitation was not from an earthly king, but from the heavenly King. Our invitation said, "*Come unto me all you that labor and are heavy laden, and I will give you rest.*" That is our royal invitation! He says to you and me, "*Follow me and I will make you to become fishers of men.*"

The lyrics of the old hymn appropriately declares, "*I heard the voice of Jesus saying, Come unto me and rest, Lay down thy weary one, lay down, thy head upon my breast.*" That refers to the invitation. Then comes our response, "*I came to Jesus as I was, weary, worn and sad, and found in Him a resting place, and He has made me glad.*"

Our invitation is also a developmental invitation. But because we are in a developmental process is why the songwriter penned these words, "*Please be patient with me, God is not finished with me yet.*" Our testimony is we are not what we want to be, but I thank God we are not what we used to be. It is a developmental invitation that's why every round goes higher and higher. The message of this chapter of David's life shows how God can arrange, maneuver and orchestrate events in our development that will prepare us for our future destiny.

A CHALLENGE FROM THE VALLEY OF ELAH

Chapter Four

Samuel 17: 1-11

The battle of David and Goliath is one of the favorite stories in the bible for many Christians. It represents the obstruction that can block our opportunities. This battle illustrates that opportunities are sometimes wrapped and packaged up in some kind of difficulty and in order to experience the opportunity we have to dispose of the obstruction. In fact, often times this is what separates achievers from non-achievers.

Non-achievers don't get past the difficulty to experience the blessings that are available on the other side.

Sometimes we will face small opposition and at other times we will face large opposition, but whether small or large the opportunity always equates to the opposition. The larger the opportunity is the larger the obstruction will be. The bigger the risk, the bigger the reward will be.

This text presents a custom that was a common Eastern practice in Bible days. That is, armies would select one representative warrior for a showdown contest. It was not uncommon for disputes to be settled in this manner. Actually, it is not such as ancient practice as it seems.

At the last Winter Olympic games all of the participating countries sent their representative athletes. And when our representatives won in a certain category we said, "We won." Or, when our representatives lost in a category, we are obliged to say, "We lost."

Goliath was the single obstruction facing Israel that day. And, sometimes advancements in life will be blocked by just one thing! Just one thing can separate a person from true greatness.

Have you ever seen someone who would have been terrific if it was not for one thing? Sometimes it is alcoholism, but it could be a myriad of things. I remember an excellent seamstress who worked in an all men's store. She was the absolute best at alterations that I have seen in my life. The problem was that she was an alcoholic, and one day I went there for service and she was no longer employed.

This was an actual case that proves a person can be separated from greatness by only one thing. Sometimes it is a personality deficiency that keeps us from being great. There are people who are enormously gifted and tremendously talented, but they lack the perception and discernment for substantive social interaction. And, they do not realize that they are in their own self's way. They are so oblivious to the truth that they are their own worst enemy. Furthermore, they play psychological games with themselves by blaming others for their shortcomings. They also cast the blame for their failures upon other people. The sad reality is that they prevent themselves from the greatness to which God is calling them.

Internal problems can prevent us from gigantic achievements as well as external problems. Nevertheless, Goliath represents the external obstruction that can prevent a Christian from experiencing true greatness.

The Challenger (Size)

You cannot help but see that Goliath was a huge obstruction. His height was "*six cubits and a span.*" We don't use that measuring technique today, but suffice it to say that Goliath was over nine feet tall. And, the hint in the text is that his weight was comparable to his height. In addition to his height he wore a "*coat of mail*" (a vest or breast plate) and it weighed five hundred shekels of bronze. This was really "a big dude." Furthermore, "*the staff of his spear was like a weaver's beam*" and the spear's head weighed six hundred shekels of iron. And that's not all: he had an armor bearer in front of him who was not much smaller than he was. A challenger would first have to get past his armor bearer before he could have the privilege of a contest with Goliath.

A conclusion can be drawn from the analogy of this battle, which is that the Lord will on occasion allow us to face an obstruction far bigger than we are. And, if we do not know something about God, if we do not know a little bit about the ways of God when we are facing a gigantic obstruction, if we do not know how God works and what He is doing, we will collapse in confusion or even lose our faith.

God sometimes permits us to come up against stuff that is bigger than we are to force us to rely on Him. It is His way of causing us to realize that we need him. The fact is that we can feel fairly independent of God on occasion, so we have to be taught and taught over and over again that we need Him.

There is a secret to David's confidence in facing Goliath. David's confidence really did not come from the fact that he took a bear down the other night. Neither did David's confidence come from that fact that he took a lion out the other day. The secret to his confidence was that he knew Goliath was God's fight, not his.

A peek ahead will reveal where David got his confidence. He says in verse 47, "*and all this assembly shall know that the Lord saves not with the sword and the spear,* **for the battle is the Lord's**." This was long before God told Jehosaphat, "*the battle is not yours, it's the Lord's.*" David knew something about how God would help His people to do battle with a larger opponent. We have God's help with any situation that overwhelms us. You are not in the midst of your trouble all by yourself. Whatever your trouble may be, the Lord is with you. If it is marital, God is with you. If it is your family (unruly children), God is with you. If it is a financial dilemma, God is with you and has a solution. Simply put, whatever the case may be, especially situations that are bigger than we are, we need to know that the battle is the Lord's.

Goliath was a huge, towering warrior. He came from a warring, barbaric people. He came from Gath, a city in Philistia. The Philistines had been enemies of Israel since the days of Joshua. But, because he was such a huge warrior, he was also a huge target.

We used to say back in the day, "the bigger they are, the harder they fall." That's fine, as long as they don't fall on you. Sometimes, our experiences will be to encounter something that is bigger than we are. As it was with Israel in this text, many times the path to a blessed destiny is blocked by some kind of obstruction. Sometimes it is blocked naturally, sometimes satanically, sometimes financially, and sometimes numerically.

The Challenge (Serious)

This was a serious challenge. The challenge that Israel faced from the Philistines represents the satanic challenge that the people of God face in any generation. That is why Paul said, "*For we wrestle not against flesh and blood, but against principalities, against spiritual wickedness, against the rulers of darkness in high places.*" Furthermore, that is also why he said, "*Put on the whole armor of God.*"

It is called the conflict of the ages: the contest of good against evil, and right against wrong. There is a satanic foe that is dedicated to the destruction of everything that is good and of God. We saw the bare backside of Satan on September 11, 2001. The Lord had introduced him as the one who comes to steal, to kill and to destroy. That description fits the work that caused the devastation on that day.

Please understand that psychic readings are not Satan's true intent. To tell you where you can find some money, or to tell you how find a lover is not his true intent. He is trying to bait us in with a psychic reading, or a palm reading. When he cannot make us worse than we are, he will use his energies to keep us from *becoming better than we are*. Do not miss that! His *only* goal is not to just take you *down*. His *other* goal is not to let you go *higher*. His goal is not necessarily to make you *worse*, but to keep you from getting *better*. That way we will not look for new destinies. We will not think of improvements beyond where we are now or what we are doing now. We will not dream of God taking us places where we have never been before, nor will we think of being something we have never been before.

I learned a poem when I was a boy in my little country school. It goes like this, "*Good, better, best, never let it rest till the good is better and the better is best*." Good is not good enough. Whenever we are striving to *be more* for God and *to do more* for God, we will be challenged. Not only will there be opposition, and not only will the opposition be strong, sometimes it will not be a silent opposition.

Goliath was strong, true enough, and he was not silent either. He talked a whole lot of "smack" down there in the valley. After hurling insult after insult at the army of Israel, he then challenged them to send him a man – a macho man to fight with him. He tried every insulting thing imaginable, but there was no response to his challenge.

Later on we will discover that he presented himself forty days, morning and evening. A total of eighty times! However, he did not put on all his armor to walk silently in that valley. He was talking "trash."

The military terminology for what Goliath was doing is called psychological warfare. It is what the Japanese did to us during World War II. Their psychological warfare was not only carried out in the prison camps, but also through a personality know as Tokyo Rose. With her honey-dripping, fluent, English-speaking voice she taunted, teased and humiliated our troops. It had a devastating affect on their moral.

Likewise, the words of Goliath demoralized Israel's soldiers. However, of all the emasculating and humiliating insults shouted at them, the most serious and the most damaging words are in verse 9. "*Let him fight with me and if he kills me, then will we be your servants.*" But, watch the twist: "*If I beat him, you will serve us.*" The price of defeat was high, and the cost of victory was even higher, making this a serious challenge indeed.

Furthermore, we can conclude that there are Goliaths even in our day. There are Goliaths who have defeated many a well-intentioned person through negative, discouraging talk. Many a person with good intentions has had to listen to a Goliath spewing out negative responses to every positive plan that was being discussed.

The Goliath of sarcasm has taken out many who had begun their walk of faith with God. The Goliath of criticism has defeated many who aimed straight at the target of success. The Goliath of cynicism has destroyed many who had focused themselves toward a goal that would honor God.

General Colin Powell did not become the first African American Joint Chief of Staff by listening to criticism. He had to beat down criticism.

Mae Jemison, the first African American woman astronaut, had to disregard a whole lot of nay sayers.

Jackie Robinson would not have become the first African American World Series MVP if he had not turned a deaf ear to the Goliaths of his day. When he came to bat, there were no cheers. There were boos, sneers, jeers, and ethnic epithets being called out to him from his own team's fans. So the conclusion then is this: if we make it at all to the destiny that God has designed for us, we will have to make it over someone's criticism, over someone's cynicism, and over someone's negative speculation. And if you can't take it, you wont make it!

The Cowardess (Shame)

The Bible says, when Saul and all Israel heard the words of the Philistine, they were dismayed and greatly afraid. Dismayed equates to discouraged. That is a terrible combination: to be discouraged and scared.

I have been discouraged many a time, but if I became *discouraged* and *scared* I would need prayer as never before. We would have no more forward progress as a church. No pastor can lead God's people while discouraged and scared. 1 Samuel 17:11 connects to chapter, 16:14. That is where it says, "*the spirit of the Lord had departed from Saul.*"

The explanation for those words is the reason for Saul's fear. Without the accompaniment and empowerment of the Holy Spirit, fear took total control of Saul's life because faith and fear cannot coexist. One will put the other out of business. Either faith will put fear out of business, or fear will put your faith out of business. They cannot "hang together" – one or the other has to go.

The Bible says, "*God has not given us the spirit of fear.*"

What's more, Saul's fears were transparently transmitted to his army. When they saw that their leader was scared, their bravery faltered. Lest we forget, Saul was head and shoulders above anyone in Israel. He was their biggest man, and if he would not go fight the giant what do you think his subordinates were going to do?

What a shame, here was Israel, the people whose God is from *everlasting to everlasting* and they are trembling in fear; the people whose God neither *slumbers* nor *sleeps* and they are hiding and hunkering down in a cave; the people whose God *measured the waters in the hollow of His hand* and *meted out heaven with the span*, who *comprehended the dust of the earth in a measure, weighed the mountains in scales and the hills in balances*, and they are scared! Their God was known as a battle-axe in the time of war. It is obvious that they had no need to be afraid.

In the next scene, David arrived at the camp and modeled the faith that is needed to overcome the challenge that they faced.

He approached the battlefield alone.
He accepted the challenge to fight the giant alone.
He stood before the giant alone.
He fought the giant alone.
That is, humanly speaking he was alone.

The New Testament parallel is given by the Apostle Paul, who wrote: "*If God be for us, who can be against us*?"

The story continues past the portion of scripture that is designated for this message. And the life-like application is we should not let our own experiences end on a negative note. We can take God at His Word. We can hold on and cling to every word of promise that the Lord has made to us. He will fight our battles if only we will keep still. And we should not fight our battles in our own strength, but we should fight in the strength of our Lord as exemplified by David.

COURAGE TO FACE THE CHALLENGE FROM THE VALLEY OF ELAH

Chapter Five

1 Samuel 17: 12-37

Courage was the foundation beneath David's victory over Goliath. Courage was the reason why David defeated Goliath. If we are to be victorious over the giants that challenge us in our day, we will most certainly need to have courage. As you can see, 1 Samuel 17 is a lengthy chapter. However it is not only lengthy, it is a very rich narrative – and being Old Testament Scripture, it is full of pictures of New Testament truths.

The Old Testament illustrates many great truths that were later completely developed in the New Testament. The conflict between Israel and the Philistines represents what is called the "conflict of the ages." That is, the conflict between right and wrong, and between good against evil. Ultimately, it is God and Satan in conflict.

The text is one of the many battles that took place between Israel and the Philistines, but the difference with this battle and the other battles is that this battle took place in the territory of Israel. We would say that this battle took place on "Israel's turf."

The opening verse of the narrative identifies the place of this battle. It says, "*they gathered at Socoh which* **belongs** *to Judah.*" Socoh was an area in Israel, which is further evidenced by the fact that David could walk rather effortlessly from his home to the place of the battle. This means that the Philistines had encroached far inside of the borders of Israel.

That is significant! It is one thing for us to be in Satan's territory, which is bad in its own right, but it is worse still when Satan invades our territory. What's more, Christians need to realize that he is not hesitant about invading our space. He is not above invading your harmonious family. He is not above invading your marriage, and he is not above invading the church. So this battle represents Christians in spiritual warfare. Consequently, we are admonished in the words of the Apostle Paul to "*put on the whole armor of God.*" He tells us why: "*That you may be able to withstand all the fiery darts of the devil.*"

Back in the days of Moses and Joshua, God had commanded that Israel was to go into Canaan and possess the land from the Canaanites. But the Philistines were there when Israel arrived and they were intending to stay there. Now, there is no need for a scientific analysis, or a geometric explanation, for what will happen when two objects attempt to occupy the same place at the same time.

A collision will occur!

We know what happens when two automobiles, or when two airplanes, or when two trains try to occupy the same place at the same time. The same thing happens when two armies attempt to occupy the same place at the same time: conflict occurs.

Another analogy of this battle is that it represents the inner conflict of believers. It represents the external invasion of Satan. However, our warfare is not only external, it is internal as well. When we receive Jesus Christ as our savior, we are given a new nature. But make note of this: the old nature that was there before the new nature arrived intends to stay there! And again the Apostle Paul addresses the frustration of the two natures in Romans 7. He wrote, "*I want to do good, but evil is present. Sometimes, instead of doing good, I find myself doing what is wrong.*"

It is the conflict that goes on in every Christian. He described it and discussed it in great detail. It is the personal battleground of all Christians.

Please understand there was more at stake in this battle than mere victory or defeat. This was not like a sporting event. In January of 2004, our city (San Diego) hosted the biggest sports event of the year – Super Bowl XXXVII. The Super Bowl is the biggest sports event in American culture and the simple summary of that event is, *a team won and a team lost*. Of course, the team that won received more money than the team that lost. However, the difference between the Super Bowl and this battle is there was an unseen spiritual dimension interwoven and intertwined in this fight. It is described in verse 9 where the challenger said, "*Do you have a man who can fight with me?* **If he wins against me, we will serve you, but if I beat him, you will have to serve us.**"

That describes the spiritual dimension of the battle. Winning and losing is a lot different in spiritual matters than non-spiritual matters. When we win for God it is *great consolation*, but when we lose there are *great consequences*. That's a lot different than winning or losing a sports contest.

The Background Movement

The more I study the Word of God and see how God interacts and intervenes in human events, the more I am intrigued by God's background movement. God can be a spur-of-the-moment God if He wants to be. God can be a right-now God whenever He feels like it. God can move in a hurry whenever He pleases.

But another viewpoint that I would like you to have of God, and appreciate about God, is that often times God works far in advance of the showdown time. God is often working long before we realize that He is working. When we have what we call our "drop-dead dates," when we have to have all the pieces of the puzzle together, when we need all of our ducks lined up in a row, when the money has to be on the table or the deal falls through, and God shows up and delivers our blessing, we need to understand that God did not start working on our problem that morning. He had been at work long before. When God comes through at what seems like at the last minute, He has already been working a long time in the background!

I love the story of Elisha and his servant, Gehazi, the one when the King of Syria decided to send a detachment of soldiers to capture the prophet. You must understand that the Syrian army was the dominant military force at that time, and the King of Syria dispatched "horses and chariots and a great host" to take one man. They encircled the city of Dothan where Elisha lived, and when his servant got up that morning to take care of his morning chores, he saw the Syrian army surrounding the city. He rushed back to tell Elisha, and said, "T*hey have come to get us and there is nowhere for us to hide.*"

And Elisha prayed, "*Lord, open the young man's eyes that he may see that those who are with us are more than those who are against us.*" And when the young man looked again, he saw that God had been at work in the background of the night. There were angels standing on the inside of the circle of the Syrian army. The angels had swords drawn in their hands to protect Elisha and his servant from the attack of the Syrian soldiers. Needless to say, Elisha and his servant were not taken because of the background movement of God. Like Elisha, the story of my life and ministry is replete with occasions when God was working in the background for my protection, or to deliver a victory.

The same can be said for our redemption. Yes, our redemption was complete in Jesus Christ on Calvary, but that was not when God worked it out. God had already worked it out behind the curtain of eternity, in the background! The Bible says in Revelation 13:8, that "*The Lamb was slain from the foundation of the world.*" Even our salvation is a work that God has done in the background.

So it was at the time of this text. While Israel was hunkering down, hiding behind rocks, huddling in caves, and trembling in fear at the sight of Goliath, God was working in the background. He was doing His background movement.

It is in verse 17 where Jesse called David from the shepherd field and told him that he needed him to go on an errand. David was instructed to take some food provisions to his brothers, who were soldiers in Israel's army. And the assignment included "*ten cheeses to the captain.*" That is a hint of Jesse's generosity. The point being is, of course, that Jesse's desire to send David to the battlefield was really God at work in the background.

Consider this: if David was the only person who would take Goliath out, then the equation is that David had to get to the battlefield. Skeptical folk would read that and conclude that it was a coincidence. It was not a *coincidence*; it was *providence*. This is an example of the invisible hand of God working in the background on behalf of His people.

It is important that we see God's hand in some of the most routine events that occur in our lives. A flat tire in the morning may be God working in the background of your life. Burnt toast could be God's invisible hand in your life to slow you down long enough so that you won't drive out on the freeway and be involved in an accident. When your car won't start, it may be God working in the background (unless you are one of those people who have not had a tune-up in two years). In that case, it may not be God.

If you are one of those people who haven't changed the oil in your car for thirty thousand miles, then if your car won't start that may not be God at work. If your battery is white with corrosion and looks like the snow-topped mountains in Squaw Valley, and your car does not start, it may not be God. But, the fact is that God does work in the background through some unrecognized circumstances.

God can work, and He does work, in what we may call "incidental" or "accidental" events. However, no accidents occur in the work of God! Neither is there such a thing as "luck." I read a fascinating quote the other day, it read: "Luck is when God chooses to remain anonymous!"

Consequently, every Christian ought to be able to identify some occasions when God was working in the background. We cannot take credit for what we have or credit for who we are. The fact is, we wouldn't have what we have or be who we are if God had not been working in the background of our lives. God was working when we did not even appreciate the fact that He was working. My appreciation is expressed in the lyrics of the song, "*All that I have thy hands have provided*."

Therefore, the precise meaning of Jesse's call to send David on an errand to check on his brothers was God working in the background. Jesse did not know that Israel and the Philistines had been in a forty day standoff just over the hill from his house. But, guess who did know? God knew it! So the fact is, God often uses occasional events for His background movement.

The Battlefield Match-up

The match-up was not army against army. The match-up was a one-on-one contest. The offer was presented as a challenge from Goliath, the Philistines' champion warrior. But the offer for the match-up was repeatedly declined by Israel. It was being rejected and refused each time it was presented. None of Israel's soldiers would accept the challenge to fight Goliath, including King Saul.

Furthermore, the intent of the text is for us to see that this was a **one-sided** match-up. It was an **unequal** match-up. Goliath was huge! He towered above nine feet (he was almost ten feet tall), and he had comparable weight to complete his physique. He was not fat. He was a *terrific* and *terrifying specimen*.

I alluded to this in the previous chapter: God will on occasion **permit** us to be matched up with something bigger than we are. What's more, He will sometimes **arrange** for us to have a match-up with something bigger than we are – and not just a match-up that is bigger, but sometimes a match-up that is humanly impossible for us to overcome alone.

That is the meaning of this narrative. For one person an impossible match-up may be lupus. For someone else it may be sickle cell anemia. For still another person it may be heart disease. And, for another individual it might be cancer.

However, the surprise is that you have already lived far past the deadline that your doctor gave you. You have already lived beyond your **d-e-a-d**-line and "the pun" **IS** intended. You were given a **D-E-A-D** LINE and you are not yet dead! Your own doctor calculated it for you. Nevertheless, you are still alive. Many people could give their testimony of the impossible match-ups that God has taken them through.

Someone said it is not the **size of the dog** in the fight, but it is the **size of the fight** in the dog. And there is a theological interpretation to that adage. It is in 1 John 4:4, which reads, "*Greater is He that is in you, than he that is in the world.*"

That explains how we have gotten past some of the unequal match-ups we faced. How we have overcome some of those impossible match-ups was not because of our strength, but because of God's strength. I mention this for specific observation: Goliath did not remain down in the valley while he challenged Israel. He started taunting them from the valley, but he did not stay in the valley.

Verse 25 indicates that Goliath began to climb up the side of the mountain to get to the top where Israel's army was hiding. The enemy is never satisfied with the territory that he has gained in our lives. He always wants more.

I do not understand how some Christians can be satisfied with the progress that they have made. If our enemy is never satisfied with what he can stop us from accomplishing for God, then we should never be satisfied about what more we can accomplish for God. Notwithstanding, often times there is not a giant blocking us from making forward progress. Many times, it is our own complacency. Many times it is our own mediocrity. However, if you are facing an unequal match-up, be assured – and reassured – that God is your equalizer.

The Bravery Manifested

In order to take down an unequal match-up, we will need to manifest some bravery. The truth of that statement is in an old song we used to sing: "*God don't want no coward soldiers in his band.*" God can't use cowards. Cowards can't hang out with God. David manifested bravery.

There are at least three kinds of bravery. First of all, there is foolish bravery. Then there is **fleshly bravery**. And, finally, there is **faithful bravery**.

Foolish bravery is just that…foolish! It is "bravery" that does not count for anything. Some time ago there was news coverage about some teens in another county. They played a game to see who could stand the longest in front of an approaching train. And, the foolish conclusion is that the person who could stand the longest as the train drew closer was pronounced the "bravest". That is dumb and foolish! It has been reported that a couple of the young people have been injured. If that is fun, it is foolish fun.

Fleshly bravery appeals to our ego. It is when something is done based on a dare. The dare to take drugs is nothing but fleshly bravery. I do not have to prove to anybody how brave I am by shooting dope into my veins, or sniffing powder up my nose. The results are obvious.

Third is faithful bravery. This is bravery that is rooted in faith. This bravery comes out of faith. It is bravery that has been birthed into existence by faith in God. The first hint of David's bravery is in verse 23. "*As he talked with them, behold there came up the champion, the Philistine of Gath, Goliath by name, out of the armies of the Philistines and he spoke the same words as before* **and David heard them**."

The hint of David's bravery is in the closing words of that verse: "*And David heard them.*" They were the same obscene, vulgar words that Goliath had spoken for almost six weeks, morning and evening. The difference this time, of course, was that David heard them. The Israeli soldiers had heard them, but their response was to run.

However, David's response was to ask, "*What is going to be done for the man who kills the giant?*"

Saul had introduced an incentive plan for the person who would kill Goliath. It was three-fold. One, he would make him rich. Second, he would give the man his daughter Michal in marriage (No one knows how much that enriched the incentive because no one knows what Michal looked like). The Bible usually describes good-looking women. However, there was no physical description for Michal.

Lastly, Saul would make the father's house of the man who killed Goliath free. That means no taxes for the family of the man that took out the giant. Not to have to pay taxes would amount to a tremendous savings for any household.

David's inquiry about what would be done for the man who killed Goliath revealed his balance between *spiritual revelation* and *physical reward.* David could see the spiritual connection of the battle, which no one else could see. Insight into the spiritual nature of the battle gave him balanced appreciation about the reward.

This is the balance shown in the words of Jesus when he said, "*Man cannot live by bread alone.*" The meaning is, we need physical nourishment as well as spiritual nourishment. In that regard, some Christians are out of balance spiritually. The old adage says they are so heavenly minded that they are no earthly good. Furthermore, some Christians are out of balance in the opposite direction. They help themselves to treasures here on earth. Their philosophy is to get all you can and to can all you get, and sit on the can and poison the rest so no one else can get any.

But David was balanced. He had insight that this was spiritual warfare as well. He also knew this was not Israel's battle alone, that it was the Lord's battle – and knowing that reduced the threat of the opposition. It does not matter what the size of the opponent is when you know you have God on your side.

Notice this about bravery. Bravery can be transparently transmitted the same as fear. Saul had transparently transmitted his fear to his soldiers. That is why no one would go out and take on the giant. But, when David took him down, Saul's army rose up and they chased the Philistines to the gates of Ekron. They got brave because David was brave.

A leadership principal can be taken from this occasion: no people can rise above their leader. No church can rise above its pastor. A leader can rise above his people, but the reverse is never true. So here was the basis for David's bravery. It was not in the fact that he had previously taken out a lion. Neither was it the fact that he had previously taken down a bear. His testimony was: "*The Lord who delivered me out of the paw of the lion, and out of the paw of the bear, He will deliver me from this Philistine.*"

I hope you see the source of his bravery. It was not in his own skills, but in the presence, power and ability of God! His bravery was attached to the words, "*The Lord will deliver me.*" David knew that the battle was the Lord's, and not only the **battle**: David knew that the **victory** would also be the Lord's.

The lesson that we should learn from this battle is that our problem is God's problem. Whatever difficulty we may experience, that difficulty is God's difficulty. I can only speak for myself: I am going to use the example of David to face whatever giants come up in my pathway. I am going to use the strength of the Lord and not my own strength. I would strongly suggest that when you have to tackle something bigger than you are that you not go against it in your own power, but rely on the power of God. No victory will be achieved if we fight with human weapons. "*The weapons of our warfare are not carnal but mighty in God unto the pulling down of strongholds*" (2 Corinthians 10:4). The victory belongs to God because the battle belongs to God.

CONQUERING THE CHALLENGE FROM THE VALLEY OF ELAH

Chapter Six

1 Samuel 17:38-54

The lessons that can be taken from this ancient story are many and the applications are numerous. They serve as examples for Christians in modern times. This story *confronts* us about the faith we do not possess and *confirms* us in the faith that we do possess. It encourages us in our own conquests with gigantic matters. It is a story for the *faint of heart* as well as for the *faithful heart*. It encourages the discouraged and reaffirms the resolved.

However, we should note that God is the foremost personality on display in this story, not David. It is about David indirectly, but it is about God directly. It shows the interaction of human reliance with God's resources. It is an example of how we can take on issues that are bigger than we are. It exemplifies how we can take on problems, and even people, who are bigger than we are. The story forewarns Christians of the occasions when we will have to deal with trepidations of life that will be bigger than we are.

In the last chapter we highlighted the *courage* of David, but in addition to his courage it is equally important that we underscore his *companionship* with God. Actually, if we were to rank his companionship with God over and against courage from God, we would have to rank companionship first. His courage came out of his companionship with God. David deepened and sweetened his companionship with God during the times of solitude provided by the long, lazy hours when he was tending sheep in the remote areas of Bethlehem. And that is an indication that we should nurture our companionship with God.

We should also guard our companionship with God. And we should take special interest to cultivate our companionship with God. If our companionship with God is close and strong, then when the big challenges come they will not devastate us. When people collapse under the weight of some gigantic crisis, it is an indication that their companionship with God is not as healthy as it should be.

Prior to the battle with Goliath, David's reliance on God was tested by a lion, and later by a bear. We should be aware that our reliance on God most certainly will be tested from time to time. There is progression in the challenges that David encountered. First, he had to deal with the lion; second, the bear; and third, Goliath. Learn this truth about God: God will test us first for the new destinies that awaits us. As we consider the theme of this book, Discovering the Destiny of David, we would be wise to know that great destinies will be preceded by great tests. The lion, the bear, and Goliath were increasing tests to prepare David for his destiny as King of Israel.

My wife, Betty, tells of her experience as a young first-level secretary with the County of San Diego. She was unable to attend college, so lowered her preference and enrolled in business school to train as a secretary. Her first job came equipped with a mean-spirited, prejudiced supervisor who either wanted to make her quit, or was trying to fire her. Consequently, this woman nit-picked and scrutinized every piece of work that Betty prepared. Keep in mind please, those were the days before computers were commonplace. She did not have the convenience of "spell check" or the ability to "save" a document for a more suitable time to finish it. When an error was discovered, the entire piece sometimes had to be redone.

Nevertheless, the limitations of technology, and the berating temperament of her supervisor, ironically, became the catalysts that refined her secretarial skills. The mean supervisor was, unknowingly, preparing Betty for her new destiny as an employer. Instead of *failing*, she *flourished*. Instead of *stumbling*, she *soared*. In spite of the *berating*, she got *better*. In anticipation of the cruel and unfair scrutiny by her supervisor, Betty determined to work more conscientiously and skillfully.

Well, guess what? Several years later there was an opening for a secretary for the District Chief. And, unlike some of the other departments this position called for a real first-line, top-notch secretary. She was selected after about a seven-minute interview! The assignment to the insensitive, overbearing supervisor turned out to be the "testing ground" for her preparation for advancement. In the same sense, God prepares us for new destinies day by day.

Now think about this: What if David had not taken out the bear and the lion before he faced Goliath?

We should be excited about new opportunities that prepare us for new destinies, but let's not forget that God will test us for each new responsibility. That is why so many people fail in the time of great opportunity, because they did not pass the lesser test.

David, however, was ready when the big moment came for

him. Notwithstanding, the reverse can occur and does occur. There are times when a person may have exposure to an advancement or promotion, but because he or she has not qualified with preparation the result will often be disastrous. That is what happens so many times to sports personalities who come into possession of large sums of money. Because the money exceeds their maturity, it produces devastating results.

So David had some tests that prepared him for his future destiny. God orchestrated the events that brought him to his appointment to face with the giant. Our chances are much better in dealing with big opposition when God has orchestrated the events of our life. The odds will be in our favor when God has maneuvered our life and has brought us face to face with a giant size opportunity.

However, many times God does this against our resistance. I will give you an example. The Lord took approximately three and a half years to prepare His disciples for their new destiny. Now get this! After three and a half years of preparation, one day while He was giving them an eschatological overview of the end of time, his disciples asked him, "*Lord, will you at that time restore the glory to Israel?*"

Don't miss that. He was instructing them about what was coming next on God's agenda and they were stuck where they were. They wanted the old glory days of Israel, and He was trying to prepare them for their future. Many times God gives us new destines despite our resistance.

In order to address the subject of this chapter, "Conquering the Challenge From the Valley of Elah," it is essential to mention that conquering has many and varied meanings, but the primary meaning relates to battle. It is associated with military conquests. There are additional meanings, such as to take over, or to conquer. The overall meaning is to take control. It means to subdue. And the specific meaning of this battle was to take over something that was trying to take over you. Conquering also implies, and includes, resistance to your advancement.

The Weapons

David's choice of weapons is insightful. It indicates the depth of his discernment about the enemy he was facing. David's insight and discernment relate both to the *physical dimensions* of the fight as well as its *spiritual dimensions.*

There are two dimensions of fighting in this text. One is physical and the other is spiritual. Paul tells us about this in Ephesians 6: "*We wrestle not against flesh and blood, but against principalities, against powers, against the rulers of darkness in high places.*"

He mentions it again in 2 Corinthians 10:4: "*The weapons of our warfare are not carnal but mighty in God to the pulling down of strong holds.*"

If we strategize our offense only in terms of the physical dimensions of the fight, we are going to lose for sure. If we strategize our defense only in terms of the physical dimensions of the fight, we will not have a chance. That is the reason Israel was reacting cowardly. Whenever the giant appeared, they would flee from him. All they saw was the physical dimensions of the fight. David saw more and, consequently, he understood more. He discerned that the *conflict was physical* but that the *consequence was spiritual.*

For Christian application that means whatever you are battling today, you would do better if you also saw it as a spiritual battle. That child that you no longer have control of is not just a physical battle, he or she is also a spiritual battle. Unemployment is not simply a physical matter; it's also a spiritual matter.

Moreover, whenever something has spiritual dimensions, God gets involved. Because David understood the spiritual dimensions of the battle, he refused Saul's armor. When we live by faith, rely on faith, and make decisions based on faith, we are going to look foolish to other people. In case you do not know it, the occasion will come when you are going to have to act purely on faith. And, you're going to look foolish. People are going to think you're dumb, especially in these spiritually bereft days in which we live.

David wasn't going to fight Goliath with a sword, but neither did he need Saul's armor. And, as you might suspect, Saul did not understand.

David's choice of weapons was five stones and his slingshot against a gigantic, professional killer. His choice of weapons only makes sense when you factor in the spiritual dimensions of the fight. His choice of weapons only makes sense when you also factor in faith as a weapon. His choice of weapons did, indeed, relate to the physical dimensions of the fight. He chose weapons that would give him the advantage of trajectory! His intention was to fight Goliath, but he would fight him from a distance. He would fight him all right, but not at hand-to-hand combat.

That is the same strategy that our military has adopted for the war on terrorism in Afghanistan. It is a strategy opposite to what the Russians tried to do for nearly eight years. They used ground troops with little or no affect because there are too many caves and holes in the ground in which an enemy can hide. So our strategy is to use long-range, computerized projectile bombs, and that strategy has proven to be quite successful.

David's plan was not to fight Goliath up close. Even though his choice of weapons may have looked foolish, we know they were very efficient.

The Warfare

The King James Version habitually describes the beginning of battles by saying: "*They set the battle in array.*" We would say, "*It's time to rumble.*" In our day it's, "*Let's get it on.*" Or, our terminology would be, "*Let's roll.*"

Whatever, the start of the battle can be envisioned as the first round of boxing match when the fighters circle around sizing each other up, checking each other out. The spectators were on both sides of two mountains looking down on the two opponents. However, when Goliath saw David approaching, he may have thought, "What?" The Bible says he disdained him, meaning that he had disrespect for the person being sent to fight him.

Not only did he disrespect David, he also underestimated him. I do not have to tell you of the individual athletes, or athletic teams, that have lost victories by underestimating their opponent.

The narrative explains why he disdained David. It was because he was young and good-looking. So he bellowed out, "*Am I a dog that you come to me with staves*?" That was a reference to David's shepherd staff. David was walking with the assistance of his shepherd's staff. Goliath was outraged at the sight. A shepherd boy with a stick is all that he saw. Too bad he didn't see those five rocks that David had picked out of the riverbed and put in his shepherd bag. Neither did he see God, Who was standing with David.

Goliath had an armor bearer, but David also had an Armor Bearer – the Lord God.

The spiritual dimension of the battle kicks in when Goliath began to curse David by the name of his gods. It is important to specifically note that the main god in Philistia was a stone idol named Dagon. That must have been humorous to David, because he would have remembered when the Philistines somehow captured the Ark of the Covenant during the days of Joshua. The Philistines put the Ark in the temple of Dagon, and to their surprise when their priests came into the temple each morning Dagon would be on his face in front of the Ark – and they would have to set him back up again. However, the next day when they came into the temple they would again find Dagon on his face in front of the Ark. This went on for many days until, finally, the idol fell and broke into several pieces.

So you can imagine how unimpressed David was at being cursed by the gods of the Philistines. David's response was a reference to his God. He said, "*I am come in the name of the Lord of hosts, the God of the armies of Israel whom you have defied.*" If this was only a physical battle, David could not have talked so confidently.

However, when we realize that our battles are also spiritual, we can be more confident. No matter what your battle, if you also saw it as a spiritual confrontation you could face it more confidently because you would understand that God is with you. The faith and courage of David came out in full force in his next response:

> "*This day will the LORD deliver you into my hand; and I will smite you, and take your head from you; and I will give the carcasses of all the Philistines this day unto the fowls of the air, and to the wild beasts of the earth,* **that all the earth may know that there is a God in Israel.**"
>
> (1 Samuel 17:46)

That was some big talk! He was not only talking about taking Goliath out, he was talking about taking on the entire Philistine army! That's incredible!

Notice three things about David's warfare: First, *his method*, a slingshot and a stone. Second, *his means*, the power of God! Third, *his motive*, victory for the glory and honor of God! Consider his words at the conclusion of the above verse, "*that the whole earth may know that there is a God in Israel.*" In David's mind the battle was for God's glory!

Churches everywhere, regardless of denomination, would be a different place if the people of God could get their motives straight! It doesn't matter who led what song the last time. It's sickening to watch all the pushing and pulling about who is going to be president or chairperson. No position in the church is for our personal exposure. The corporate efforts of the church should be that the world would know that God is at work in our lives. Christians in general will be better suited for their destinies when the glory of God becomes their purpose and motive.

The Winner

Announcing the winner of a sports contest is a formal acknowledgment. Many times it is completely unnecessary. When a guy is laying down on the floor with his mouthpiece ten feet away, and still unconscious fifteen minutes after the referee has counted him out, then here comes the announcer for the official announcement to say, "and the winner is…"

My goodness everyone can see who the winner is! An announcement is not needed in that case. When Goliath went down like a fallen tree, it was obvious whom the winner was. David ran to the giant. All the other Israeli soldiers had been running from the giant. Faith will make you advance and fear will make you retreat. David's maneuver was so swift and skillful that he was standing about five feet from Goliath winding up his slingshot before the giant knew what happened. And, before he could blink a stone struck him in the forehead with the force of a bullet.

David hurled the stone, but God handled the stone.
David slung the stone, but God steadied the stone.
David threw the stone, but God targeted the stone.

"*And the stone sank into his forehead and he fell down upon his face to the earth.*" David then ran and stood up on the giant and took his sword and finished the job. This was the fulfillment of David's brave words that "*God will deliver you into my hands.*"

In a previous chapter, I mentioned that faith could be transparently transmitted to others the same as fear. That is precisely what happened. The army of Israel rose up from their hiding places and chased the Philistines all the way to the entrance of Gath and the gates of Ekron.

Their response to David's victory reminds me of the television game show called *Family Feud*. When the representatives of a family win the game, all the other family members run and jump up on stage and start celebrating. However, you notice that the losers do not have other family members jumping up on stage. A similar reaction took place when David took out Goliath. Many times when there has been a great victory in the church people who haven't been fighting will join the celebration as if they helped deliver the victory.

Finally, for the sake of the person who may have a giant size challenge in his or her life and has been responding in fear and despondence, I simply want to lift up this narrative as evidence of the power of God. It shows us how the power of God can work behind and within human faith. Whatever you may be facing, it is not too big for God. If you have the faith, God has the power. God can take it down, no matter what size it is. God can take it out, no matter how large it is.

LIFE AFTER THE GIANT

Chapter Seven

1 Samuel 18:1-16

David's life was never the same after he defeated Goliath. In a single exploit of courage and marksmanship, David was ushered out of obscurity forever. He would never know again the silent Judean hills of Bethlehem. He would never experience again the quiet solitude as he shepherded his father's sheep beside still waters and into green pastures.

In a single moment he had gone from obscurity into popularity – and our challenge is to realize that it was a tremendous life changing transition. It is one thing to reach another level of destiny, but it is quite another thing to reside at a new level of destiny. We must be aware of the difficulties that accompany staying at a new level of living.

As we anticipate and appropriate levels of our destiny we must also be aware that it is not necessarily easy to stay at new levels of living. Human nature being what it is and as it is, most people can stand a lot more adversity than they can popularity. Popularity brings a whole set of new problems with which to deal. Praying comes easier when we are *struggling* than when we are *soaring*.

However, David is our model for appropriate adjustment at different levels of the latter of destiny. He had what it took before advancing to each new level. His *courage* led him to this new level, but his *character* enabled him to stay there.

The story is told of a gentleman who wanted to climb a mountain. So he hired a guide and, sure enough, after several grueling hours of climbing they finally arrived at the top of the mountain. He immediately gave in to the temptation to stand up to see the vast expanse and the extended horizon that the height of the mountain made it possible for him to see. And as he was just about to reach his full height, his guide snatched him down to his knees and said, "The only way you can stay this high is on your knees. The wind current will blow you away."

It is not uncommon for people to make it to the top, but often times they don't have the inner quality to stay. David was an exception! He possessed the qualities for each new level *before* God promoted him to the next level. Likewise, he models for us the qualities we should possess *after* being promoted to another level.

Please note precisely that the single quality and the qualifying factor in David's life was his deep personal relationship with God. David had a deep personal relationship with God when he was in *obscurity*, and he maintained that relationship with God after gaining *popularity*.

President Franklin D. Roosevelt described the attack on Pearl Harbor on December 7, 1941, as "the date that will live in infamy." A similar description could be given of the day that David defeated Goliath. The two opposing armies witnessed the defeat of Goliath. The Philistines looked on in *disbelief*, but Israel looked on in *delight*.

Not only did David win an extraordinary victory that day, he also won for himself a loving friend. From the time of the defeat of Goliath, to the time David was crowned king – who, including his preparation and testing time, was approximately sixteen years – Jonathan remained his beloved friend.

David's Loving Friend

God, who knows the constitutionality of our frame and who knows and supplies all our needs, knew that it was essential for David to have a loving friend after taking out Goliath. Considering all that he would be exposed to, and all that he would experience and go through, God provided for David a personal, loving friend. David would, after defeating Goliath, be looked upon by *admirers*, but also by *adversaries*. *Delighted* eyes would behold him, as would eyes that despised him. Consequently, a loving friendship was indispensable for David.

What can compare to a genuine, time-tested friend? As a boy growing up, I was often warned by my parents to "be careful of the friends that you make." Even the Lord Jesus was not excluded from the company of personal friends. Of the twelve disciples, there was the "inner circle" – Peter, James and John. But in addition to them, there was the home in Bethany occupied by Mary, Martha and Lazarus where he frequently withdrew from time to time for refreshment, relaxation and to recompose Himself. The grief of losing friendship with someone that was nurtured by years of intimacy, the friendship of someone that you absolutely trusted, confided in, and become personally transparent with, is equivalent to the loss of a loved one. David and Jonathan had that kind of friendship, and it was never lost.

The other day I read an interesting description of a friend: "A friend is another self." Jesus alluded to that when He said we should love our neighbors as we do ourselves. A friend is someone who knows you and who understands you; that is, knows your weaknesses, knows your faults and knows where all your bad spots are and still loves you anyway. That is a true friend!

Considering someone of David's stature and position, it would be even harder to attract a genuine friend and develop an authentic friendship. Public figures find it difficult to attract genuine friendships because often times it is difficult to determine the genuineness of the motive of the person who is attempting to be their friend. It is easy to look at people for *what they have* rather than for *who they are.* A famous person has even more difficulty acquiring genuine friendships, but David and Jonathan had a classic friendship and it is worthy of our emulation today.

Note the basis for their friendship. It is worth our discovery and our discussion. It is described in the first verse of chapter 18: "*It came to pass when he ceased speaking unto Saul* (David was talking to Saul while holding Goliath's head in his hand) **that the soul of Jonathan was knit with the soul of David and Jonathan loved him as his own soul**." There is more in the third verse: "*Jonathan made a covenant with David because he loved him as his own soul.*" There is the basis for a true friendship!

People must connect *internally* before they connect *externally.*

This is the description given in Deuteronomy 13:6. The Lord was warning Israel about false gods and said, "*If your brother, the son of your mother or your son or your daughter or wife of your bosom or your* **friend who is as your own soul**..."

The remainder of the verse continues with the warning about false gods. However, it's hard to find a more apt description of a friend than someone "*who is as your own soul.*" A recent adage gives the description as a "*soul mate.*"

Plainly speaking, the way the word "*love*" is used in the friendship of David and Jonathan makes people of our western culture uneasy, primarily because we only have a one-dimensional meaning, or understanding, of the word "*love.*" There is a recent movement underfoot in some Christian circles advocating acceptance of homosexuality as an alternative lifestyle. This push to accept homosexual couples is based on the friendship of David and Jonathan, and in particular on how the word "*love*" is used to describe their relationship. The misunderstanding comes from a misinterpretation of 2 Samuel 1:26. David was lamenting the death of Jonathan and said, "*I am distressed for you my brother Jonathan, very pleasant have you been unto me.* **Your love to me was wonderful, passing the love of women**." It is these words, in particular, that are misinterpreted. The mistake is in not knowing that the Greek language has three words for *love* - in English there is only one.

In John 3:16 when we read: "*For God so loved the world ...*"

The Greek word for love is **agape**. The definition for agape is how an act is performed for someone. The second Greek word is **Eros**. That word does not appear in the Bible. However, from it we get our English word *erotic*. **Eros** is sexual love. Then there is **Phileo**. **Agape** and **Phileo** appear in John 21, when Jesus asked Peter, "*Do you love me*?" Jesus used **agape** in the question, and Peter used **phileo** in response. **Phileo** is friendship love. The English meaning would be to like someone. Actually, this kind of love (**Phileo**) can exist between two people of the same gender as well as people of the opposite gender. It is the purest form of love because it is a sexless relationship.

David said Jonathan's love surpassed the love of women. In no way, and at no time, has God ever intended for sexual acts to occur between people of the same gender. Ironically, it is the homosexual point of view that homosexual sex surpasses heterosexual sex. That is an absolute affront to the creative design of God. In no way can that be true because too much is missing in homosexual sex. When a man is with a man, too much is missing! When a woman is with a woman, too much is missing! God had something in mind when he made a man for a woman and a woman for a man!

Unfortunately, because of the permeating homosexuality in our culture, people have to be very careful when they initiate a friendship with someone of the same gender because they may be looked upon with suspicion, as if the friendship is not truly genuine. But, a person doesn't have to be "funny" to have a friend of the same gender. The text says that David and Jonathan made a covenant, and that is common between friends. Friends make covenants!

David and Jonathan's covenant appears in chapter 20, verse 14. The words are from Jonathan: "*You shall not only while you yet live show me the kindness of the Lord that I die not.*"

Those words or in the covenant because the common practice in those days was for the incoming king to kill all the heirs of the outgoing king. So Jonathan asked David to "s*how me the kindness that I die not.*" He continues in verse 15 and 16:

"*But also you shall not cut off the kindness from my house forever. No, not when the Lord has cut off the enemies of David, every one from the face of the earth. So Jonathan made a covenant with the house of David saying 'Let the Lord even require it at the hand of David's enemies.'*"

Jonathan extended his request to include his descendants: *You shall not cut off the kindness from my house forever.*" That was the covenant!

Furthermore, Jonathan gave David gifts. Gift giving is not uncommon among friends. He gave David a robe and he gave him his sword, he gave him a bow, gave him his belt, and other garments. David was poor. Saul had never made him rich, as he had promised, for taking out Goliath. Consequently, he had no tangible gifts to give back to Jonathan. His gift to Jonathan was to honor the covenant they had made and he did that when he was seated and settled as the new king of Israel.

With his scepter in his hand one day he commanded his subjects to see if there were any descendants of the household of Saul alive so he could bless them. Only one was found. He was Jonathan's son and his name was Mephibosheth. David decreed that Mephibosheth would live in the palace and eat daily at the king's table. Thus, David honored his friendship with Jonathan and kept the covenant they had made.

For all the years leading up to his kingship, David needed a friend. God provided him such a friend in Jonathan. People whom God singles out for destiny will need friends in their lives.

Jonathan became the eyes and ears that David needed and was his confidant until the end. Furthermore, Jonathan was instrumental in saving his life several times.

David's Longtime Foe

In contrast to a loving friend, David had a longtime foe. King Saul became David's archenemy. David *supported* Saul but Saul was *suspicious* of David. It was really strange how Saul turned on David. Actually, the person who gained the most from the defeat of Goliath was King Saul! It was **his army** that won the victory after Goliath was slain, not David's army. It was **his kingdom** that was vindicated by the death of Goliath, not David's kingdom. And, David was **his servant**.

Unfortunately, an insecure character flaw beset Saul. He was threatened to the core by the excellence in David. We can walk away from this narrative with loads of inspiration for our personal application. The contrast of the weaknesses of Saul to the strengths of David is packed with relevant meaning. Out of their eschewed relationship we learn the value of taking a personal reality check. The blatant boldface truth is that everybody is not going to like you. Period!

I had not been a pastor for six weeks when I realized I was not going to have one hundred percent loving support from the congregation. And, I discovered that people don't need a reason not to like you. They just don't like you. That's all! For every good thing you stand for and represent, they can think of three bad things. They expect you to treat them right, but they won't relate the same standard in return. They will act like they have a license to treat you anyway they want to treat you, but you had better treat them right. It is not uncommon that the people you help the most will hurt you the most.

Two influencing issues fed Saul's character flaw and his resultant treatment of David. They were envy and jealousy. For sure those ingredients are a dangerous combination. You are in for the heartache of your life when you have to interact with someone who is reacting to you out of envy and jealous contempt. Jealousy is when you do not want someone to get what you have. But envy is when you want something that someone else has. When those two negative attributes are working together in someone that you have to interact with, you are in for trouble.

Both of these negative personality traits were working overtime in Saul's treatment of David. Nevertheless, the sardonic fact is that Saul loved David! That is said in chapter 16:21. He loved him and hated him at the same time. His envy of David was manifested by the response of the people to David. Chapter 18:6 says, "*And it came to pass as they came when David was returned from the slaughter of the Philistines that the women came out of all the cities of Israel, singing and dancing to meet King Saul.*"

David was admiringly welcomed when he returned from leading the army against their enemies. But, as if that wasn't enough to set Saul off, the women made up a song that took him over the top. They danced and sang, "*Saul has killed his thousands and David has killed his ten thousands.*" It was only a fable tune, and the first fact about this fable – if there are facts about fables – is that Saul had not killed a thousand of the enemy and David had only killed one person. But Saul's reaction could not be suppressed. The eighth verse says, "*And Saul was very angry.*"

At that point anger got in the mix. Add some anger with some jealousy and some envious contempt and you have some disastrous consequences headed your way. You may know someone who is functioning out all three of those emotions. This is the person that other people will have to tiptoe around. This is the person that you have to choose your words carefully with because he or she will "fly off the handle" at the "drop of a hat."

The ultimate escalation of envy, jealousy fueled by anger, is to hurt or to harm. The ultimate escalation of jealousy is to hurt emotionally, that is why it is called verbal abuse. This is when a discussion about apples and oranges turns into an argument and the desire is to inflict pain – not physical pain, but emotional pain. It is accomplished by making personal references that will result in pain.

The next step in the escalation is the desire to inflict actual physical pain. The intent is no longer to inflict pain emotionally, but also physically.

The third step in the escalation is to not only inflict pain physically, but also permanently! Saul tried to kill David at least twice: once with a javelin and later on with a spear.

Hopefully, the ultimate escalation that we may encounter is an altered version of physical pain resulting in permanent injury. Usually the permanent injury does not occur often. Thank God! However, a person's influence can be killed. Attacking or undermining someone's pure motive can do it.

Let me point out one more negative factor that was functioning in Saul's life. We have already noted envy, jealousy and anger. The other is fear! Verse 12 says, "*And Saul was afraid of David.*" So, because he was afraid of David, he removed him from the palace and made him a captain over a thousand men. However, that really wasn't a promotion. Saul's motive was clear. The end of verse 17, says, "*Let the hand of the Philistines be upon him.*" That was his real motive for "promoting" David over a thousand men. It's even clearer from the end of verse 25: "*Saul thought to make David fall by the hand of the Philistines.*" It was a peculiar kind of fear. There is the fear that will make you run from someone that you are afraid of, and there is the fear that produces the motivation to kill the person who is feared. It's a peculiar kind of fear.

Andrew Hacker makes a reference to this kind of fear in his book *Two Nations – Black and White, Separate and Hostile.* He points out that the imbalance of arrests in black communities and the imbalance of incarceration from black communities is not because there is really more crime in black communities, but because of fear. It is a reaction to fear of the black man.

We already have the psychological evidence that all the lynching that took place in the late 1800s and early 1900s were because of fear. The arrest and incarceration of black men, in particular, is the replication of the same kind of fear that perpetrated the various lynching.

At the same time that David was subjected to the jealous hatred of Saul, the narrative shows that all the people in the kingdom accepted him. Verse five says, "*He was accepted in the sight of all the people and also in the sight of Saul's servants.*" And verse 16 says, "*All of Israel and Judah loved David.*" The final summation comes in verse 30, "*His name was much esteemed.*"

This proves that something was drastically wrong with Saul's perception of David. The conclusion is that anyone who did not love David had to work overtime to find something unlovable about him. His name was much esteemed; that is, until Saul got through working his mischief. David was fine with everyone until Saul began a negative campaign against him. You may have heard the statement that a lie won't hurt because it is an untruth. Well, that's a lie! It just depends on who is telling the lie. A lie that is told by the right person about the right thing at the right time can do damage for a lifetime.

What Saul did to ruin David's reputation could happen to your family, in your church, at your school, and especially in the workplace. The Lord speaks to the negativism of this text when he tells us "*Bless those who curse you. Do good to those who despitefully use you and pray for your enemies.*" The only way David survived Saul's mistreatment was because of his close personal fellowship with God.

David's Lasting Fellowship

I have already alluded to the fact that David had a close personal fellowship with God. It is wise to have a "tight" relationship with God when people start chewing you up and spitting you out. You had better make sure you know how to call on God when folks start "ragging on you." Otherwise, you will not be able to take it. How David reacted to Saul's hatred is proof of his lasting fellowship. It is mentioned four times that David "*behaved himself wisely before Saul,*" meaning that he said all the things he was supposed to say and never said anything he was not supposed to say while in the King's presence. Neither did he do anything that he wasn't supposed to do when he was before the King. While in

Saul's presence, he behaved himself wisely.

However, a closer examination of verse 30, shows a difference to the other three references to his behavior. This verse says he behaved himself **more** wisely. The other three times the references indicated that he was wise, but the fourth time he was "more" wise. Christians need to realize that God is in the "more" business. Jesus said, "*I am come that they may have life and that they may have it* **more** *abundantly.*"

God is in the "more" business, I tell you. Jesus said, "*Every branch that bears fruit is pruned so it will bear* **more** *fruit.*" Jesus said, "*If you know how to give good gifts to your children how much more will your heavenly Father give.*" Out of all the shenanigans that Saul tried to pull on David, David still grew *more.* He developed in wisdom more. Furthermore, he gained more strength.

There is inspiration for us to discover from this ancient text. The lesson you need to take from this story is to know that God can bless you in the midst of your adverse circumstance. You do not have to move anyway. That old hymn we used to sing years ago is still true. God will fight your battles if you will keep still (and keep your mouth shut, too).

Here is how this narrative speaks to me. It indicates that it does not matter who is mistreating you. It does not matter who has mistreated you. Some of us have got our heads down about things that occurred twenty years ago. God can find a way to deliver you a blessing in your situation and if He can't find a way, He can make a way. The odds can be stacked against you but it won't matter. Opposition can manifest itself in gigantic form but the God that I serve and before whom I stand has power to protect and deliver you.

God can bless you in the midst of an inequitable situation. David is the model! He never raised a hand against Saul. God was his defense and defender.

TARGETED FOR DESTRUCTION

Chapter Eight

1 Samuel 19:1-18

The title for this chapter proposes a chilling thought but a real truth. David was targeted for *destruction.* However, another truth is hidden behind that truth, and it is that he was also targeted for *destiny*. The distinction is that the One who targeted him for destiny was not the one who targeted him for destruction, but it explains why he was targeted for destruction.

People who have been *tapped for destiny* will often be *targeted for destruction* and, if not for destruction, at least for *distraction*. David, no doubt, was unaware that two poles were at work in his life and, likewise, each of us should be aware that two poles are at work in our life. The description for theses two poles is found in Romans 7 where Paul says: "*What I should do, I do not want to do, and what I should not do is what I want to do.*" What Paul described is the spiritual struggle that occurs in every believer.

While watching one of the launches of the space shuttle, and listening to the commentary between astronauts and the people at the controls in the space center, I also saw an excellent example of the Christian's spiritual struggle. When the shuttle reaches a certain height, it is subjected to two gravitational pulls. At a certain point, it is in the pull of Earth's gravity that is pulling it backward. However, at the same time it is also in the pull of the moon's gravity that is pulling it forward.

Christian living is like that. Destiny has a pull on our lives, but distractions are pulling on our lives at the same time. We hear two voices; one saying "yes" and another saying "no." One voice says, "You can do it" and another says, "You better not even try." In addition to our inner struggle to be more than we presently are is the external pressure to distract us or to destroy us. Saul represents that external pressure in David's life.

What David experienced at the hands of Saul is a shadow of what Jesus experienced at the hands of His enemies. When the Lord was at the peak of His ministry is when His enemies worked hardest to destroy Him. "*Then the Pharisees went out and held a council against him how they might destroy him*" (Matthew 12:14).

Saul's numerous attempts to take David's life illustrate the evil at work to keep us from being all that we were meant to be, as well as to prevent us from doing all that we are meant to do.

The four negative motivations that culminated in Saul's contempt for David were enumerated in the previous chapter. There was *envy, jealousy, anger,* and *fear.* His mean-spirited acts toward David were not *occasional* attempts to destroy David; they were *continual* attempts. Saul ruthlessly pursued David for approximately sixteen years.

Have you ever wondered how, or why, a person is able to stay angry for a long time? Ever wonder how people can be obstinate and mean for a long periods of time? The answer is an evil spirit! Long-term anger, obstinacy, and meanness are not gifts of the Holy Spirit! Anyone who can stay mad for extremely long periods of time has to have help. No one can stay mean alone. The assistance to stay mean and mad will come from satanic motivation and inspiration, as demonstrated by King Saul. What is portrayed in this tragic story is a sustained satanic effort by Saul to destroy David. Moreover, a big piece of David's life was absorbed while he was fleeing from Saul.

The Public Intention (Desire)

In a previous chapter we saw that the intention to destroy David was a private motivation of King Saul. Two times he attempted to strike David with his spear, but they were private attempts. His motive was private when he made David the captain over a thousand men. His private hope was that David would be killed as he engaged the enemy. His request for David to kill one hundred Philistines to win the hand of his daughter in marriage was another sly private attempt to endanger David's life.

For the record, the Bible shows that David killed two hundred Philistines in half the time he was given to complete the assignment. However, all that did was make Saul angrier and more determined to destroy David. Obviously private motivations are not the same as when they are made public. Public motivations are another level above private motivations.

Hitler could have privately held all of his barbaric, inhumane, anti-Semitic notions and the world would have never known the difference. However, the world was changed forever because his private intentions became public intentions. Public intentions of destruction will often include other people. Sometimes an assailant will work all alone, but at other times coconspirators are recruited. That is the essence of verse one. Saul told his son Jonathan and all his servants that they should kill David.

Human nature has not changed since the days of this text. Human nature has not improved since the time of Saul. People are capable of that kind of behavior in our time. For example, it can happen in the workplace, not necessarily physical destruction but destruction in the sense that a person can be forced out of employment by a variety of ingenious actions. It can also happen in school and at church. I repeat, not necessarily physical destruction, but the destruction of a person's ability to reach God-given potential. In the church it is called spiritual destruction.

The warning from this ancient text is that you should guard your emotions so that you never become a leader in organizing or orchestrating a group to destroy someone. Not only should we guard our emotions so that we do not become a leader, but we should guard our emotions so that we do not become a follower of a leader who is organizing and orchestrating a group to destroy someone.

Be wise!

Be discerning!

Know when you are being recruited to destroy someone.

The inspirational and enlightening fact is that Jonathan refused. He would not be recruited to destroy David. At the risk of being the recipient of Saul's rage and wrath, Jonathan said "no." Jonathan's refusal indicates that any relationship or friendship must have some boundaries. Friendship needs some parameters. The parameters guard what we should and should not do in a relationship or a friendship.

Proverbs 21:6 says "*Faithful are the wounds of a friend.*" A friend is supposed to tell a friend what is right even if it wounds him or her. You do not need a friend who will get mad at someone just because you are mad at that person. You do not need a friend who will strike out at somebody just because you want to strike out at that person. That is not a description of a true friend.

Jonathan did not say "no" to a friend, but rather to his father, the king – and then he persuaded Saul against his own intentions. Verse 6 says, "*Saul hearkened unto the voice of Jonathan and Saul swore as the Lord lives that he shall not be slain.*" Granted, it was a short-lived, momentary persuasion, but he persuaded him nonetheless.

Subsequently war broke out between Israel and Philistia again, and David was the hero again, not by himself this time but as a military leader. He and his division of soldiers fought gallantly. What's more, they got all the glory for the victory, too.

You know what that did to Saul? It set him off again! Verse 10 records his third attempt to kill David with his spear.

The Pursued Implementation (Design)

Ill-informed and ill-intentioned messengers set out to implement Saul's design to destroy David. It's one thing to *desire* the destruction of someone, but it's quite another to *design* the destruction. Also, it's one thing to *possess the intention* of destroying someone, but it's still another to *perform the implementation* of that destruction.

Some people not only conceive the destruction, they can actually carry it out. These messengers represent pure, unadulterated duplicity. This is duplicity at its lowest depth. To *plan* destruction is one thing, but to *pursue* the destruction is altogether different.

Now let's be honest. We have all entertained the idea of "getting" someone. We have all considered the thought of "doing someone in" or "doing someone up." I do not know what is worse – being *done* in or being *done* up. Nonetheless, at one time or another we have all thought, "I ought to do this to him or do that her."

The difference is we never pursued the thought. Somewhere between sunrise and sunset the Holy Spirit reminded us of who we are and Who's we are. I know it has happened to you because it has happened to me. But what was about to happen to David is different. It is the follow-through that few people have the stomach for. It's one thing to plan to destroy someone but quite another thing to see it through.

A while ago I watched an intriguing movie on television that had tremendous historical perspective. The movie was about twenty-five handpicked Nazis who gathered in a house way back in the woods. Twenty-five handpicked Nazis met to plan the annihilation of Jews in Europe. Many of them were military people. There was a sociologist among them, a scientist, and an engineer. The entire movie took place in the dinning room of a large mansion, except for a few scenes that were shot outside near the house.

While the discussions were going on about the biological affect that gas would have on people when used for extermination purposes, some of those guys got sick to their stomachs. Dyed and tried Nazis became nauseous. Jew-hating Nazis got up from the table under the pretense that they had to go out and smoke and vomited! One person got up from the table under the pretense that they needed fresh air and went out side and threw up. Another went to the restroom under the pretense that he needed to use the toilet and got sick. Jew-hating Nazis could hardly stand to hear the plan of gassing millions of people.

But this text shows us that some folks have the stomach for it. Some people have what it takes to carry out the threat. They are mean enough to execute the plan to the last detail. The plan to destroy David was not done in self-defense or in response to a threat that they had received. David had done nothing amiss to warrant this kind of behavior.

Perhaps this incident was the inspiration for David to write Psalm 59. The inscriptive heading says, "*To the chief musician, Altashheth, Michtam of David when Saul sent men and they watched the house to kill him.*" It is very likely that this psalm was written out of the background of 1 Samuel 19. Look at verse 1: "*Deliver me from my enemies O God; defend me from those who rise up against me. Deliver me from the workers of iniquity and save me from bloody men, for lo, they lie in wait for my soul. The mighty are gathered against me not for my transgressions, nor for my sin O Lord. They run and prepare themselves apart from any fault of mine. Awake to help me and behold.*"

However, when Saul's henchmen arrived at David's dwelling his wife played a trick on them. She helped him escape in the middle of the night and made a dummy-like image and placed it in his bed to make it appear as if he were there. She put some goat hair up on top and apparently did a good job.

Now the first time I saw this trick was when I was a boy watching a Roy Rogers movie at the Leon Theater in downtown Pleasanton, Texas. Roy Rogers used that same trick. He took his blanket and put his hat up at the top, put his boots down at the end, built his campfire up real high, slipped back into the darkness, and made Trigger be quiet. When the bad guys came they shot up the blanket, and when they came to see where their shots had landed he came up out of the darkness and captured them.

After I grew up, I found out that Roy Rogers was a devoted Christian. Maybe this Scripture is where he got that idea. He may have read it in the Bible, but the point is that it worked for David and it worked for Roy Rogers, too.

Verse 18 says, "*So David fled and escaped.*"

The Providential Intervention (Deliverance)

David fled and escaped, but notice to where he fled. He fled to Samuel the prophet! The Bible had been silent about Samuel since the day he anointed David as King. After that he drifted into the background of the narrative. Approximately two or three years had passed since that notable event took place.

David ran to Samuel not so much for *physical protection* but for *spiritual preservation*. He needed to hear a word from the Lord through the man of God. After all, commission from God will often require confirmation from God.

Have you ever had to go back before God for confirmation about something He wants you to do? Your prayer may go something like this, "Now Lord, I know you said for me to do this, so why is it so hard for me to get it done? I know you wanted me for this job, but why am I running into so many brick walls?"

We pray like that because we need confirmation for what God has told us to do. In those cases we are having what I call a faith building experience. God uses circumstances to strengthen us for what He has called us to do. David was actually being strengthened for his coming role as King.

Remember what the Lord did for Gideon who started out with thirty-two thousand soldiers in his army? When God finished testing his men for battle he only had three hundred men left to go to war.

That was a faith builder.

A faith builder teaches us to rely totally and completely and absolutely on God. Understand this, David would become the most loved King of Israel; and not only the most loved, but also the best-known King of Israel. He would become the best king that Israel ever had, period! He would become the *pivotal prominent progenitor* in the lineage of Messiah. Of all the hundreds of progenitors in the lineage of Messiah, Jesus is called the son of David! Therefore, with credentials like that he would certainly need to know how to trust God. So with that kind of notoriety facing him he needed to know how to put his trust completely, totally, and absolutely in God.

First of all, you have to be whom God wants you to be before you can go where God wants you to go. God *allows* some things to occur in our lives and He *disallows* some things from occurring in our lives. On the one hand, God *permits* some things to happen, but then on the other had He *prohibits* some things from happening.

Now, look at the graphic description of David's dilemma. The person who was hunting him down had the most civil authority in all of Israel. It was the King himself! I will attempt to make it plainer. What do you think it would be like to be hunted by the FBI? Where would you run if the FBI were trying to kill you? Where would you run if the CIA were trying to kill you? Are you getting the picture? You need to have a sense of David's hopeless situation to appreciate his deliverance.

When Saul found out where David was hiding, he sent *messengers* to his location who actually were *murderers*. He sent three different groups of "messengers" on three different occasions. Their purpose was to kill him, but they couldn't do it on any of those occasions. Why? Verse says, "*Saul sent messengers to take*

David and when they saw the company of the prophets prophesying and Samuel standing as appointed over them, the spirit of God came upon the messengers of Saul and they also prophesied."

Samuel had taken David to Naioth to one of his prophet training schools. He had five schools of the prophets at various locations. That is where they were hiding when Saul's messengers arrived. However, these messengers not only heard the Word of God, they started speaking the Word of God themselves. It was sort of like what happened when some guys went to arrest Jesus. When they found Him they pulled out their pistols and cocked the hammers back, but they couldn't go any further. Consequently, they returned empty handed. The authorities asked them, "What happened? Why didn't you get Him?" And their response was, "*Never have we heard a man who speaks like that man.*"

This is an example of some of the ingenious ways God has to deliver us and protect us. The Word of God stopped them! There are people who curse God's name everyday. They have no consciousness toward God, but there are some things that they will not do because of the Word of God.

I used to have a friend who would come by and leave offerings for the church. He was a gambler and he would always tell me, "Now, Pastor, this is good money. I would not bring you gambling money." The man did not know God, but had enough respect for God's Word not to give gambling money to the church. The record is clear that the Word of God stopped these messengers from getting to David.

It was, indeed, a peculiar incident for these guys to prophesy and speak the Word of God. However, it is not necessary that we know what God is doing, it is only important that we know that He is doing it.

This case is similar to what happened in Numbers 22 when Moses was leading the Israelites through Moab and Balak, the king of Moab, did not want them to go through his land. So he hired a prophet named Balaam, and he instructed Balaam to curse the people of God so they could not continue on through the land.

Balak brought his prophet up on one side of the mountain so he could have a good view of the people of God, but as Balaam started to pronounce a curse he was, instead, moved to pronounce a blessing on God's people. Balak determined that Balaam didn't have a good enough angle from that side of the mountain, so he took him to another place on the mountain and asked him to curse the people from there. Once again as the prophet began to speak blessings came out. What we are to learn from both of these occasions, perhaps, is the sovereign intervention of God on behalf of His servants.

After the messengers had gone back and forth three times, Saul accompanied them the fourth time. Verse 22 says, "*Then he also (that is Saul) went to Ramah and came to the great well that is in Sechu and he asked and said 'Where are Samuel and David?*'" And, someone was more than willing to tell him. "*O king, they ran to Naioth,*" was the response Saul received for his inquiry. The narrative continues at verse 23: "*And he went there to Naioth in Ramah and the spirit of God was upon him also as he went on.*" Watch this now. Saul had not gotten near to their hiding place when be began prophesying and speaking the Word of God. He was still in route when "*the Spirit of God was upon him also as he went on.*"

Earlier I alluded to how peculiar this incident was. That is the best adjective I have to describe it, peculiar! It is uniquely peculiar for a person who does not know God to speak the Word of God. But, it may not be as peculiar as it seems when compared to some of the words God has made you say and some that you didn't intend to say. You had in your mind how you were going to tell someone off and when the occasion came around, you could not say the words. You were like Balaam. You were going to cuss, but you could not say the words. So it is not as peculiar as it appears. Notwithstanding, the essence of this phenomenon is that good is superior to evil! Good has more power than evil.

It is difficult to explain how this affected Saul. Verse 24 indicates that Saul stripped himself down to his underwear and lay on the ground day and night. Strange indeed! Nevertheless, it could have the following meaning: pure satanic evil in an individual clashed with the pure good of God, and evil lost. It is something like what occurs when a person who is attempting to jump-start a car accidentally attaches the positive jumper cable for the negative battery pole. What happens? Sparks fly in every direction! Consequently, the instruction for jump-starting a car is that the positive cable should never touch that negative battery pole. That might very well illustrate what happens when pure satanic evil in a person comes into contact with the pure good of God, and that might be what happened to Saul.

Unfortunately, Christians in our time would look at Saul lying on the ground stripped to his underwear for a day and a night and ascribe worshipful significance to it. They would make it an acceptable worship occurrence. It is happening in congregations all over and is called "slain in the spirit." The more bizarre behavior people display in worship, the more significance is ascribed to it.

Some facts to consider about this incident are: 1) no one else was lying naked on the ground but Saul; 2) the other prophets who prophesied were not on the ground naked; 3) Samuel was there and he wasn't lying naked on the ground; and 4) David was there and he was not on the ground naked. In fact, no one was naked on the ground for a day and a night other than Saul!

The question that was raised about this incident comes at the end of verse 24. "*Is Saul among the prophets*?" What is the answer? A resounding unequivocal, *No!* Not in the sense that he had become a prophet. He was among them, but *not of them*. I repeat, what this narrative shows is simply the ingenious ways in which God can protect and deliver his own.

While Saul was lying on the ground, chapter 20:1 says, "*And David fled from Naioth and Ramah*." He went back to Jerusalem. David was nobody's fool. While Saul was lying on the ground for a day and a night, David gathered up his stuff and took off. It was not a permanent reprieve, but permanent enough for him to get away again.

That is the essence of this narrative – God can and will protect and deliver His own. That ought to provide assurance for every Christian. We don't have to know why God is doing what He is doing; we just have to know that He is doing it. How God chooses to protect and deliver us should be no concern of ours. The way He chooses to protect and deliver us is no concern of ours. All we need to know is that God will protect and deliver His own.

DODGING DESTRUCTION

Chapter Nine

1 Samuel 20:1-17

If we learn any truth at all from David's encounters with Saul, it should be that God *provides* for His own. If there is a message that we should hear from this narrative, it is that God *protects* His own. Furthermore, we see in this narrative that God can use our mistreatment by others toward us for our own maturity.

Unbeknown to David, God was strengthening and deepening his spiritual maturity through his mistreatment by Saul. David, obviously, did not know it at that time and he certainly did not appreciate it at that time, but the fact is God can wring good out of evil for our benefit. David learned that later. He learned that truth after the fact as we often do.

As we are going through a trial or through some testing experience it is difficult to see the work of God's providential hand. However, just remember that God is always working His perfect will for our benefit. God can turn *blunders* into *blessings*. He can make *stumbling blocks* into *steppingstones*.

The classic testimony of God's power to reverse evil and mistreatment is Joseph's testimony when he said to his brethren, "*You meant it for my harm, but God meant it for my good.*" The fact that God can reverse bad circumstances should help us to live more faithfully and confidently as Christians.

At the time of the text, David was far from the man and servant of God he would later become. This proves a peculiar truth about how adversity works to strengthen us at the core of our character. Notwithstanding, no one wants adversity and when it comes it is not welcome in our lives. I have not heard of anyone who believes in the practice of "naming and claiming" who have named and claimed any kind of adversity. Nonetheless, it is true that adversity strengthens us for service unto the Lord.

This narrative also shows the deep depth of cruelty that can be resident in human behavior. Not only does it reveal the depth of cruelty resident in human behavior, but also the depth of cruelty that can be released through human behavior. Saul was eaten up with envy toward David and he was relentless in his attempt to destroy David. Consequently, David spent much of his time dodging destruction by running from Saul.

The Fugitive's Peril

A fugitive who innocently flees is a person dodging destruction, and here is what we must remember; that while David was a *fugitive* from Saul, he was also favored for service. That balances the scales and evens the score! He was a *desperate fugitive* but he had *divine favor*.

I strongly believe that Christians would not collapse so easily under the weight of their trials if they could remember who they are, Who's we are, and Who is on our side. We have the Lord's promise that He will never leave us nor forsake us. I do not know about you, but it lightens my load to know that the Lord is with me. Because of the Lord' presence, our burdens are not our burdens alone. He is with us through all our trials.

One day David woke up and found that his life was in peril and he described his desperate state as being one step ahead of death. At the time of this text he had returned to Gibeah. He had previously fled from Gibeah and had gone to Ramah and then on to Naioth to be with Samuel. However, he came back to Gibeah again for comfort and consolation from his friend, Jonathan.

Once he was back in Gibeah, David told Jonathan how Saul had sent "messengers" to kill him. And, he also told him how Saul eventually came himself to personally kill him. But, Jonathan did not believe him. Jonathan said, "My father is not after you. If he intended to kill you, I would know it. I'm his right hand man. I am next in line to be king. I am his heir. He is not after you David."

Notice Jonathan's concluding statement at the end of verse two, "*It is not so.*" It makes me wonder where Jonathan had been all the while David was running away. It appears that he was out of the loop concerning the King's intentions toward David. And, that was essentially David's reply to Jonathan. He said, "Your Dad knows that you and I are the best of friends. That is why he is keeping it from you."

Note this please: Jonathan did not know because Saul had not told him. That explains his ignorance about Saul's intention to destroy David. Jonathan apparently based his statement on Saul' promise to him that he would not kill David (19:6).

There is a second reason why Jonathan did not know; David had not told him. That is one of the many qualities we are going to see in David's character, which come to the surface throughout his lifetime. I do not know many people (Christians included) who have been offended by someone and did not tell someone else about it.

They have to tell somebody!

But not David; he didn't tell Jonathan or anyone else that Saul wanted to kill him. Nevertheless, perhaps in a patronizing tone, Jonathan said as recorded in verse 4, "*Whatever your soul desires I will do it for you.*" There is no mention of how David felt about Jonathan's reluctance to believe his father wanted to kill him. However, he devised a plan to secure his safety from Saul.

The Fictitious Proposal

David was required to dine at the King's table on the first night of the new moon, which was the next evening. But David was not planning to be there! Dodging Saul's javelin three times had convinced him that the king really wanted to kill him. And, not only did Saul attempt to kill David three times, he had three times also sent messengers to do the job. So on six different occasions Saul had attempted to take David's life. Consequently, David was convinced that Saul intended to kill him.

I think I would have been convinced long before then. In fact, I would have been convinced after the first throw of the javelin. However, David teaches us something about people who have good character and people who are good-natured. It's hard for good-natured people to see bad in someone else. It takes them a long time. They almost have to be run over by a truck before they know someone intends to harm them.

But, watch out for folks who have bad natures. They see the bad in everyone and everything all the time. Perhaps you have been in conversation with someone who says, "You know, I sure do appreciate him and what he does," and then another person will say, "Well, if you knew what I knew you wouldn't say that." Or, you may compliment someone by saying, "Oh, I just love the way she sings; it is so spiritual and uplifting," but the person you are talking with may say, "If I told you a thing or two about her you wouldn't feel that way."

The fact is that people with ugly dispositions see ugly things in other people. David was slow to realize that Saul wanted to destroy him. It took six attempts on his life before he finally got the picture as to Saul's intention.

Still, he couldn't stay away from the King's table without permission, or without an explanation. So he rehearsed a fictitious proposal with Jonathan and it went like this: "*If I am missed at the table and the King inquires about me, you say that you gave me leave to go to Bethlehem for a family feast. If the King is not angry, I know I can return. But if he is angry, I will know I must continue to flee for my life.*"

That was the plan. Jonathan agreed and David continued to say to Jonathan, "*You have brought your servant into a covenant*" (David saw himself as Jonathan's servant). That is another of the many God-like qualities of David that floats to the surface. Don't miss it, please.

Samuel had already anointed and pronounced him the next king over Israel. And, although he was going to be the next king, he saw Jonathan as his superior! He continued by saying to Jonathan, "*If the king is angry when you tell him I went to be with my family, I want you to kill me.*"

That statement is a description of David's *desperation, exasperation*, and his *frustration*. He was ready to give it up. He couldn't take it anymore. He had nowhere to run, no place to hide, so he wanted Jonathan to end it all for him. As far as he was concerned, he had reached the end of his rope. He was tired of running for his life. It was all over for him.

It's amazing how much more we can take after we think that we can't take anymore. It is amazing how much more you can do after you are convinced that you have already done all that you can do. It is amazing how far you can go after you have said you have gone as far as you can go.

I will never forget when I was about to graduate with my Bachelor of Arts degree. I had been in college for such a long time. To give you an idea of how long it had been, it took me six years to get a two-year degree. Anyway, we had measured for our caps and robes and on the way back to class I told my good buddy, Dick Smerud, that I was going to pitch a fit if I had to take one more class.

Well, guess what.

A few days later I was called to the office and informed that a check of my records revealed that I was one class short! The news was devastating! However, I didn't stretch out on the grass and kick and throw a fit as I had said I would do. I was permitted to participate in the graduation ceremony, but I had to return the next semester to complete my last class.

It is amazing what we can do, and what we can take, after we have said we can't do anymore or take anymore.

David managed, by the grace of God, and with protection from God, to stay at a safe distance from Saul for another sixteen years. But, he thought it was over when he was talking to Jonathan.

Let me share with you the words Winston Churchill spoke at an academy graduation, "Never, never, never, never, never, never, never, never, give up!" That was all he said, and then he turned away from the podium and went back to his seat. I would modify his words slightly and say, "Never give up on God."

The Faithful Promise

The faithful promise was Jonathan's response to David's request for him to take his life. Jonathan assured David that if his father definitely wanted to kill him, then he would send him away to safety. However, you will notice that Jonathan was actually speaking to God while making his promise to David.

Let me clarify this for you. In the culture in which Jonathan and David lived a promise was serious business. Consequently, they would actually address their promises or vows to God. "*As God is my witness*" was a common Old Testament phrase. Furthermore, there was a time in our culture when we took our promises more seriously than we do now. There was a time when we used to say, "cross my heart and hope to die" before we made a promise. And when we said those words the person to whom we spoke could be sure that we meant what we said.

When was the last time you heard someone say "cross my heart and hope to die?" We would do well as a people to have more integrity about the promises that we make.

Verse 13 is Jonathan's promise to God and verse 14 is his covenant with David. He began his response to David by addressing God with these words, "*O Lord God of Israel...*" However, at verse 14, the covenant was addressed to David. Jonathan essentially said, "I will use my royal position to protect you and save your life, but when you eventually come to the throne, you must use your royal position to protect my life and my house."

The significance of Jonathan's statement is that he had accepted God's will for David to be the next king of Israel! He had accepted David's *promotion* over his *demotion*. That is incredible considering that Jonathan was next in line to be king after Saul! It was through his spiritual discernment that he knew God was not going to carry on the kingship through Saul's linage.

Believe me, there are a whole lot of hand-clapping, foot-patting, head-nodding, body-rocking, dancing-in-the-aisle Christians who couldn't do that! Some Christians can't rejoice when another Christian receives advancement, particularly if they don't also get advancement. Jonathan's spiritual maturity in Old Testament time had developed far beyond some Christians in our time.

So Jonathan told David, "*Stay here three days and on the third day, come and stand by the stone Ezel. I will shoot three arrows toward the stone and if the arrows fall short of the stone that will mean it is safe for you to remain in the King's service. However, if the arrows sail past the stone that means it is not safe for you to stay. You must flee for your life.*"

The first night Saul missed David at the table he did not say anything. The end of verse 25 reads, "*and David's place was empty.*" Then in verse 26 it says, "*Nevertheless Saul spoke not anything that day for he thought something had befallen him or that he was not clean.*"

Saul's thoughts about David's absence from the table give insight into his insecure and selfish nature. The statement really means he hoped that something unfortunate had befallen David, or that he was unclean.

I alluded earlier to people who have good natures and how hard it is for them to see bad in other people. The opposite is true of people with bad natures. They easily imagine bad things about people. Saul's thoughts about David prove it.

His first thought was that something bad had happened to David; then with his wicked imagination he refined it into the possibility that David was unclean. Without any evidence whatsoever, he concluded that David was absent because he was unclean. (Refer to Leviticus chapters 5 through 15 for the sanitary laws of Moses for when a man was unclean or a woman was unclean).

First of all, Saul thought (hoped) that something tragic had befallen David. Then he amused himself by thinking that David was unclean because of some sexual activity. Unfortunately, too many Christians are like Saul. They are the arresting officers, the jailer, the prosecutor, the judge and the jury. They convict and condemn without a shred of evidence. It is a sad reality that the spirit and mentality of Saul is existent in people today.

One night had passed and there were two nights to go, but the next night at the King's table things didn't go so well. Saul missed David again on the second night, and this time he inquired of Jonathan about his absence. He asked, "*Why is it that the son of Jesse hasn't come to the table neither yesterday nor today.*"

It would be interesting to go into the psychological and sociological implications of why Saul did not call David by his name. He referred to him anonymously as the "*son of Jesse.*" However, we can conclude that it superficially gratified him to depersonalize David. Nevertheless, Jonathan responded with the words of their fictitious proposal. He said, "*He asked permission of me to go home to be with his family and I granted his request.*" And verse 30 says, "*Saul's anger was kindled against Jonathan.*" That means he pitched a fit. He blew his stack and lost his cool.

There is a present-day movement underfoot that suggests

David and Jonathan had a homosexual relationship. This movement is pushing to make homosexual relationships an accepted alternative lifestyle. Furthermore, the movement is not only from outside the church, it is from inside the church as well. Verse 30 is the so-called "proof" for their twisted conclusion. It is taken from Saul's response to Jonathan, "*You son of a perverse, rebellious woman! Do I not know that you have chosen the son of Jesse to your own shame and the shame of your mother's nakedness?*"

Note that the key words in the text are "rebellious" and "shame." The King James Version translates the word, "bosheth" to mean either shame or confusion. It refers to the lineage of Jonathan's birth. The reference to his mother's nakedness means that from his birth he had the right to be the next king. He was the rightful heir to the throne. "*You have chosen David but you have the right and you have chosen him to your mother's shame.*" Verse 31 really makes it plain. "*As long as the son of Jesse lives on the ground you shall not be established, nor your kingdom.*"

The meaning of verse 30 and 31 is that by choosing David he had shamed his mother. And what's more, as long as David was alive he would not become king. This indicates that Saul was aware that David would be the next king of Israel.

In his fit of rage Saul threw his javelin at Jonathan. Through that incident Jonathan knew without a doubt the intent of Saul to kill David. It says, "*therefore Jonathan knew for sure.*" There was no doubt as to what his Dad intended to do to David.

The next day Jonathan gathered up his arrows and took a little lad along with him under the pretense that he was going out for target practice. Later on in the narrative we will see the hint that Jonathan was the instructor for the archers in Saul's army, so it was not unusual for him to be seen taking off into the woods to practice with an armful of arrows. That is how he got so good with a bow and arrow.

However, he was not going out for target practice this time. Instead he was going to warn David to flee for his life. When he reached the place where they had agreed to meet, David was waiting and watching by the stone called Ezel. He saw Jonathan shoot the arrows far past the young boy, and then yell to the lad that he had to go farther to retrieve the arrows. That was the signal. As you can imagine, it was a dreaded signal to David.

The Friends' Parting

Jonathan sent the young lad back with his weapons while he waited for David to appear from behind the rock. "*David rose up out of a place toward the south and fell on his face to the ground three times.*" Bowing is the behavior of a servant to this master. David saw himself as Jonathan's servant. Bowing is the behavior of a commoner to royalty.

Next, "*they kissed one another.*" Because they kissed each other, this is supposedly more evidence to support the claim that David and Jonathan were homosexual lovers. However, in many cultures in Bible days people greeted each other by kissing on the cheek, first one and then the other. Unfortunately, what often happens is we superimpose the European culture on the Bible and often distort its meaning. That's how we have Jesus dying on Friday and rising early Sunday morning and count it as three days and three nights. We do not recognize that the Jewish day began at sundown. So the three days that Jesus was buried must be counted from sundown to sundown.

The Bible says they kissed, but it was not a romantic kiss. It was not a kiss for sexual arousal. It was the usual kiss of greeting. In fact throughout the Bible men kissed each other.

When Esau met Jacob he "*ran to meet him and embraced him, fell on his neck and kissed him and they wept.*"

When Joseph was reunited with his brethren in Egypt the Scripture says, "*Moreover he kissed all his brethren and wept over them.*"

When the Prodigal Son retuned home his father saw him a great way off "*and ran to him, fell on his neck and kissed him.*"

Kissing between men in the cultural context of the bible was done as a greeting in the same sense that shaking hands is done in our culture. On one of my trips to Israel, I had an opportunity to meet the mayor of Bethlehem. I walked into his office, and extended my hand to shake his hand, but my friend Dr. Walker whispered to me under his breath, "Kiss." So I kissed the mayor on one cheek, and he kissed me back on my cheek. And I kissed him back on his other cheek, and he kissed me back on my other cheek. So I kissed him again and he kissed me again. We went on for about four or more times because I didn't know the culture. The one who kisses first is the one who is supposed to stop. So every time I kissed him he had to kiss me back. That is still a custom in Israel today.

Not only did David and Jonathan kiss, they wept. We do not weep in our culture like they wept in their culture. David wept because he was parting from his friend, but that was not the only reason he wept. David also wept because he was losing his only friend. He had already lost his wife. Saul intentionally, and out of pure meanness, gave her to another man.

Not only did he lose his wife and his dear friend, there is no place where we see that David ever saw his father, mother or brethren again. And, that is not all David lost. He lost his reputation in Israel. And that's still not all he lost either. He also lost his good name.

Every person in Israel had their own interpretation of why David was running from Saul, none of them the same and none of them true. He had to run with nowhere to run. He had to go with nowhere to go. He had to hide with no place to hide.

His situation was like needing to dress oneself and having nothing to put on. It's like trying to sit down at the table for a meal with nothing to eat. It's like bedtime with no place to sleep.

That's what this parting was like for David. This may have been when he took his pen and dipped it in divine revelation and wrote Psalm 121:

"I will lift up mine eyes to the hills – From whence comes my help? My help comes from the Lord, Who made heaven and earth. He will not allow your foot to be moved; He who keeps you will not slumber. Behold, He who keeps Israel shall neither slumber nor sleep. The Lord

is your keeper; the Lord is your shade at your right hand. The sun shall not strike you by day nor the moon by night. The Lord shall preserve you from all evil. The Lord shall preserve your soul. The Lord shall preserve your going out and your coming in from this time forth and even forevermore."

Or, it may have been when he was inspired to write Psalm 142: "*I looked to my right and I looked to my left and I saw there was no one to help me. No one would know me. Refuge escaped me. No one would assist me. Then I cried unto the Lord. You are my help. You are my refuge and my portion in the land of the living.*"

This experience of loosing his best friend and having to run for safety caused David to trust God at a different capacity. It is not until we are at our limit that we really learn to trust God. It is when we are at our weakest, or when we have sunk to our lowest depth. Those are the moments when we truly encounter the realness of God in a deeper meaning.

God sustained David through this difficult time and God will sustain us in similar circumstances. The most important fact to remember is that when we think we're alone we're really not. It doesn't matter how strong the opposition may be we are never alone. It doesn't matter how high the mountains are or how deep the valleys we are never alone. Neither does it matter how bleak the diagnosis from the doctor may be we are never alone.

David said it best when he sang this psalm: "*The Lord is thy keeper. The Lord is thy shade upon thy right hand. The sun shall not smite you by day nor the moon by night.*"

David thought he had gone as far as he could go, but he ran for sixteen more years. We have more courage than we know when the Lord is our keeper. This was another negative experience used by the Lord to deliver David a positive blessing. The Lord was making David into the man He needed him to be when he sat on the throne of Israel. None of the kings would do all that David did as king. No other king would bless the people the way David blessed the people when he became king. The Lord had to take him low before could lift him high.

Dodging Destruction

LOOKING FOR HELP IN ALL THE WRONG PLACES

Chapter Ten

1 Samuel 21:1-15; 22:1-5

This subject carries the drift of an old once popular country western song titled *Looking for Love in all the Wrong Places*. At this point in his life David was looking for help, but he was looking in all the wrong places. In previous chapters we saw the superior spiritual qualities that David possessed. However, in all fairness it is equally right for us to recognize his inferior fleshly qualities.

David, like any other saint of God, was blessed by strengths but beset by weaknesses. Sometimes he responded wisely to the situations confronting him, but sometimes he responded foolishly. Sometimes his faith in God was strong irrespective of his circumstances, but at other times his faith in God was weak. Consequently, his motivation to run from Saul was based on his insecurity and lack of trust in God.

And, that means he ran sometimes when he shouldn't have run. He ran sometimes when he did not need to run. But, worse than his running, as a consequence of fear and because of faithlessness, is where he sometimes ran.

Sometimes he ran to Samuel, of course, which was wise. God guarded and guided him while he was with Samuel. While with Samuel, God protected him three times from the messengers Saul had sent to kill him. And, ultimately, he was protected from Saul who came personally to kill him while he was with Samuel. So he was shielded a total of four times while he was with Samuel, but it seems he ran from there on his own. He ran back to Gibeah, then to Nob, and from Nob he ran to Gath of all places.

Not withstanding, he would learn later that God was very capable of telling him when he should run and when he should not run. Later on God gave him specific instructions about when to go and when to stay. One occasion in particular is recorded in 1 Samuel 22:5. This is when the prophet, Gad, said to David, "*Abide not in the stronghold. Depart and go to the land of Judah.*" This shows that God could give him directions about when to stay or when to run.

The principle and lesson of Proverbs 3:5-6 is: "*Trust in the Lord and lean not unto your own understanding. In all your ways acknowledge Him and He shall direct your path.*" We should be careful to wait for God's directions to remain where we are as well as to wait for God's directions if we are to move on.

From this narrative we will see that God's Word does not conceal the flaws and frailties of its heroes and heroines. Their lives are transparent in the Scriptures, not simply so we can see their mistakes and weaknesses but also so we can be more aware of our own shortcomings. The truth is that we all have the same tendencies and propensities that were displayed in the lives of the people in God's Word. Let's face it; these were "fleshly moments" for David. He acted sometimes as if he had forgotten Samuel's proclamation that he would be the next king of Israel. He acted sometimes as if he had forgotten whom he was and Whose he was. And, at other times he acted as if he didn't remember God's promise to him.

Simply put, David was far from his best in this episode of running from Saul. It was bad enough for him to run to Nob, but it was worse to run to Gath in hopes of finding safety. But it's essential to remember this: when we are at our worse, God is at His best. Someone said, "When we are down to nothing, God is up to something."

Giving up when we are at our worse is not the best decision we can make. Often times we give up because we feel like we are at our wit's end. However, God is never at His end. God would have us learn more about Him out of our failures. Failure is not permanent unless we make it permanent.

I remember once failing a test in college. I mean I failed it straight up or straight down, whichever is the best description. But, during the review of the test I learned more about the subject matter than I did in all the lecture periods leading up to the test. We can learn from our failures.

In the text David had fled to Nob. This would have been a good place for him to run to if his motive had been right. Running to Nob was like some Christians who come to church. Coming to church is a good practice, but only if our motives are right. It's possible to be at church but and not in church. The content of the narrative shows that David's motive wasn't right. We will see shortly that he was motivated by fear. Furthermore, he went to Nob under the cloak of deceit and deception.

He was a Deceitful Servant

As painful as it is to admit, David acted out of pure deceit when he ran to Nob and approached Ahimelech, the priest, for help. His deceitful actions are the fate of any one who loses touch and trust with God. Furthermore, making fabrications of the truth is not uncommon for people who are trying to direct their own lives.

David pretended to be on an errand. What's more, he pretended to be on an errand for the King when, in fact, he was fleeing from the King. He asked for bread and was told that there was no common bread. That is, there was no regular bread for consumption. However, there was showbread available. Showbread was bread that was set before the Lord on the altar. It would be set out fresh on the first Sabbath day and removed on the next Sabbath day. For seven days the bread would remain there and only the priests were allowed to eat it, and they ceremoniously did in the Holy Place. The bread that remained after the priests had eaten of it was the bread that Ahimelech gave to David.

It is interesting that the Lord referred to this occasion of David when He made the distinction between keeping the letter of the Law regarding the Sabbath when it conflicts with human need. In a discussion with the Pharisees the Lord reminded them how David ate the showbread that was only supposed to be consumed ceremoniously by the priests. That's when he made the well-known statement, "*The Sabbath was made for man, not man for the Sabbath.*"

David's second request was for a sword. Somehow the sword of Goliath had ended up in Nob for safekeeping among the priests. Ahimelech gave him Goliath's sword and he left. While David talked with Ahimelech, a no-account fellow named Doeg saw him and overheard him. If you take the "e' out of his name you will say who he really was. Doeg was there because he was "*detained before the LORD.*" However, the scripture does not disclose the specific reason for his detention. Nevertheless, he will figure in the story later on.

In an attempt to improve David's image and explain his actions, some commentaries say David was really talking about himself when he said he was on the king's business. But it is futile to attempt to make David's actions before the priest noble. It's simply too much of a stretch. David did not see himself as king in this text. If he had, he would not have done what he did. But, please stand by, it gets worse.

The same is true of any person who continues to act independently of God; it cannot get anything other than worse. When anyone tries to make his or her own way without checking in with God, it can only get worse. A child of God who remains out of touch and out of fellowship with God cannot go up; he or she can only go down.

He was a Despicable Soldier

"*And David arose, and fled that day for fear of Saul, and went to Achish, the king of Gath.*"

It is hard to choose between *despicable* or *deplorable* as descriptions of David's actions before Ahimelech, and especially to explain his behavior in Gath. Actually, he was despicably deplorable when we remember the kind of soldier David was. Let's not forget that David was a famous, award-winning soldier, and here he was fraternizing with the enemy. That's treason in times of war.

David fled and went to Gath, the capital of Philistia. He went to Gath for safety and asylum. Imagine that if you can. Of all the places where he could have run, he ran to Gath. It was the capital city because the king lived there.

We should remember another Philistine warrior who came from Gath. Goliath was from Gath. Their champion whom David took out with a rock came from Gath. What chance do you think David had of sneaking into Gath incognito with Goliath's sword strapped to his belt and dragging the ground while he walked down Main Street? What chance? Slim to none is the answer. Needless to say, David was completely out of character, first in Nob, and then in Gath. He was looking for help in all the wrong places.

David's decision to hid out in Gath was both dangerous and dumb. But was no dumber or more dangerous than Christians who go into crack houses to buy drugs. It is no dumber or more dangerous than Christians who arrange for personal deliveries of illegal drugs to their residence. There is no way of knowing who manufactured the stuff. Also, there is no way to know what substance was used to "cut" it with.

And when you think about people ingesting it or sniffing it into their systems, that's not smart at all. It's dangerous and dumb. It makes David look like Einstein! Drug users make David look brilliant when walking down Main Street in Gath with Goliath's sword strapped to his belt and dragging the ground.

Actually he was not received with open welcome arms in Gath and the servants of King Achish viewed him with suspicion. "*And the servants of Achish said unto him 'Is this David, the King of the land? Did they not sing one to another of him in dances saying Saul has killed his thousands and David has killed his ten thousands?*'"

Use your imagination here. They would have known who David was even if he hadn't had Goliath's sword strapped to his belt dragging the ground when walking down Main Street. The songs that they mentioned were Israel's songs about David for his bravery and brilliance as a soldier, and the dances that they referred to were performed to honor David's achievements in battle. They knew the current dances in Israel. They also knew the popular songs going in Israel.

The question is: how did they know about the songs and dances that honored David? And how did they know that David would be king of Israel? Actually, they referred to him as king in present tense. They asked, "*Is this not David the King of the land?*"

They knew he was destined to be king of Israel because good news travels just as fast as bad news. There is an adage that says good news hasn't gotten out of bed while a lie has been around the community ten times. That is not true. Good news travels as fast as bad news. There are people who don't know God from Popeye, but they know what's going on in the churches in their communities. When any church is doing well, the unbelieving community knows it. Don't be fooled. Good news is of interest to non-Christians and unchurched people.

The reason worldly folk listen to the news about the church is because they are listening for bad news so they can have an opportunity to mock the church and say, "That's why I don't go to church." They also listen for something they can mock the preacher for and say, "That's why I don't go to church." People who enjoy looking for something to accuse the church and pastor of seem to forget that we all are individually accountable to God for our own shortcomings.

Conversely, it was improbable that the people in Israel knew much about what was going on in Gath. But the people in Gath knew what was going on in Israel. They knew somehow that David would be the king of Israel. They did not ask, "Is this not David who is going to become king?" Neither did they ask, "Is not this David who is on his way to the throne of Israel?" They saw David as king then. They had enough knowledge about the God of David to know that when God promised something it was coming to pass.

It's interesting to note that they gave David more recognition than he gave himself. They were more aware of his identity than he was. As far as they were concerned, he was already king.

It's bad when worldly folks have to remind the people of God who we are. The Scripture says, "*And David laid up these words in his heart and was very much afraid.*" It appears that when he heard the ascription of him as king, it touched his heart and brought him back to his senses. It also says he was very much afraid.

Actually, he should have been afraid long before then. It's strange that he was not scared before. He should have been afraid when he was walking down Main Street with Goliath's sword strapped to his belt and dragging the ground. That's when he should have been scared. When he walked through the gate of Gath, he should have been scared. So now he was not only afraid of Saul (that is why he ran there), but he was also afraid of Achish.

It only gets worse when we are trying to make your own way. He was afraid; obviously, the king would take revenge on him for killing Goliath. What chance did he have in case the king wanted to take revenge? What chance? Slim to none, but more none than slim.

So in self-defense, David went into a one-man performance. *He changed his behavior*. That is, he *disguised* his behavior. He went into this act while he was *in their hands*. It appears that he was in their custody. Perhaps it means they had taken control of him or had put him someplace for security purposes.

The trick was to feign that he was mad, which means he pretended to be crazy. He let saliva drool down into his beard. And he made unintelligible markings on the doors of the gate. The warning that David gives us with this acting role is that there's no telling what we may end up doing when we insist on making decisions for ourselves without God's help. The sad fact is that God may leave us to our own devices and we could end up doing despicable things to get out of the messes we have made for ourselves.

Nevertheless, we must admit David feigned it well. It worked. He did his acting job well. You may want to know how David learned to act crazy so well? Answer: he had seen Saul act crazy enough times. David knew exactly how to act like a crazy person. My goodness, he had seen Saul's crazy performances time and time again. As it turns out, he had a personal trainer, which is why he could act the part so well.

The trick worked. Achish commanded his servants to let David go, stating he didn't have need for a madman. The humorous hint is he was latently saying to his servants, "I have enough crazy people around me. I don't need another one." Chapter 22:1 shows that David departed safely from the Philistine camp.

It's interesting to discover the Psalms that David wrote out of his many personal experiences. Psalm 56 is parallel to his narrow escape from Gath. It is a *Michtam Psalm*. Michtam Psalms were written out of the background of some experience he encountered. *Michtam* means "deeply engraved." So indications are that these were songs that he wrote out of events that were *deeply engraved* in his subconscious, his mind or his soul. He wrote fourteen Michtam Psalms, all related to the time he was running from Saul. The inscription that introduces each psalm identifies the Michtam Psalms. Observe the inscription for Psalm 56. It says: *Michtam of David, when the Philistines took him in Gath.*

This psalm begins with a prayer: "*Be merciful unto me, O God; for man would swallow me up; he, fighting daily, oppresses me. My enemies would daily swallow me up; for they are many that fight against me, O you Most High." Verse three says, "When I am afraid, I will trust in you."*

He had learned, obviously, that whenever he was afraid he would from that time forth trust God and not attempt to take care of himself. It could possibly mean that while he was letting his saliva dribble down into his beard, and while he was scribbling unintelligible words on the walls in Gath, he may have been praying this prayer. It means that while he was acting crazy externally, he may have been praying internally. Consequently, it was not his acting performance that delivered him but God's answer to his prayer.

He was still desirable for Service

Despite the fact that David was a *deceitful servant* and a *despicable soldier*, he was still *desirable for service.* The emphasis is he was acceptable to God for service unto God. His deliverance from Gath also signaled his restoration to fellowship with God. Chapter 22, verse 1 indicates he was back in Israel where he is supposed to be. He was also back in touch with his family again. He escaped from Gath to a cave named Abdullah. Scripture says, "When his brethren and all his father's house heard it, they went down there to him."

This means their lives were in jeopardy just like David's life was in jeopardy. His father, who had forgotten that he had a son named David when Samuel came to anoint the king in his house, came down to be with him in the cave. His brethren who ridiculed and despised him are now with him in the cave. Notice specifically that it says, "*all his father's house.*" The people who were included in his father's house were, of course, his father and mother, his seven brothers and their wives (if they were married) and their children (if they had children). All of David's kinfolk came to him in that cave. The number could easily have been upwards of sixty people.

Seeing this massive number of family members coming to David reminds me of how careful we ought to be about writing people off for whatever reason. We must be careful whom we say we are done with. And, because the twists and turns of life can bring us back to a personal encounter with a person we said we would never need in our life again, we need to be careful as to whom we say we're going to write off. Please, just don't make those kinds of statements.

Not only did David's *family* come to him, but also *fugitives* came: four hundred men, a number that swelled to more than six hundred. They became known as David's mighty men. You can read about their personal abilities and exploits in 1 Chronicles 12.

Utilizing his God-given leadership skills, David sharpened those guys up. They were both feared and respected as fighting men. It's important to understand that these guys were products of Saul's oppressive regime. Saul's insensitive and senseless reign made them disenchanted outcasts. Consequently, they came to be with David. God used David to prepare them, and used them to prepare David. Their coming together was mutually beneficial.

That's the reason God sent him to such a large cave. It was twenty feet wide and forty feet high. God's divine wisdom is evident in sending David to this cave. Why would one man need a cave that large for a hiding place? It was because God knew that his family and all these men would gravitate to him. God sees and knows all about our tomorrows and His knowledge is accompanied by His continuing plans for us. David needed a large cave because he was going to have a large crowd with him in the cave.

One of the first things David did was to secure his family's safety. He delivered his family safely to Moab. "Why Moab," you ask? Moab was the birthplace of Ruth, David's great-great-grandmother. Therefore, David delivered his family to Moab for safekeeping among their relatives.

The following Scripture is one of the ways we can tell that David was back on track with God: "*David went from there to Mizpeh of Moab and he said unto the king of Moab, 'Let my father and my mother I pray you, come forth and be with you* **until I know what God will do for me**." He was listening to God again. He was no longer making any moves without direction from God.

First, he *secured his family*, then set about to *structure his fugitives*, and then was *shown his future*. The prophet, Gad, told him to leave the stronghold and go into the land of Judah. Because he had returned to God he was in position to hear from God again.

Psalm 57 kicks in right here. It's another Michtam Psalm. David wrote Psalm 57 from the cave, Adullam. The inscription for the heading of the Psalm says: *Michtam of David when he fled from Saul in the cave.*

Like Psalm 56 this Psalm also begins with a prayer. He says, "*Be merciful unto me O God, be merciful unto me for my soul trusts in you. Yea, in the shadow of your wings will I make my refuge.*" David's refuge was not the security of the walls of the cave, but in the shadow of God's wings. David's intention was to trust God "*until all these calamities pass by.*"

Yes, he was a deceitful servant. And, yes, he was a despicable soldier. But he was still desirable for God's service. God still had plans for his life. Those who had written him off didn't know that God would write him back in again. Those who had put David down didn't know that God would pick him back up again.

He wrote in Psalm 37, "*The steps of a good man are ordered by the Lord*" and continued to say, "*Though he fall he will not utterly be cast down*." David had experienced God's restoring grace. David was not pretty in several places in this narrative, but it is encouraging to know that God stills desires us for service even when we have been despicable and deplorable.

A CASE FOR GOD

Chapter Eleven

1 Samuel 22: 6-23

Since God can turn the mischief of others toward us into blessings for us, then it should be understood that God might also turn our mistakes into blessings for us. In the previous chapter, David was at his worst. He had reached rock bottom and it has been said that when you reach rock bottom, God is the rock at the bottom. At the time of this text, David found himself in the crucible aftermath of Saul's mischief. So David answers the question that we may ask today: "How do you resume your pursuit toward your God-appointed destiny in the aftermath of the mistreatment of others, and in the aftermath of your own mistakes?" How do you continue on to your God-appointed destiny and God-appointed destination?

First of all, we must remember that we have a God-appointed destiny and that there are God-appointed destinations for our lives. David, as you know, had a God-appointed destiny. He had already been anointed to become the next king over Israel. However, the problem with pursuing our destiny is lack of realization that we also have a God-appointed destiny.

All Christians have a God-appointed destiny.

That not only applies to people in the Bible; it also applies to people like you and me. God has a destiny designed for us. You may want to ask, "How can we know our destiny?"

In simple terms, it is God's best for you.

It may vary in specificity from individual to individual, but in general our destiny is God's best. Consequently, it should be our goal to be our best as servants of God and to *do our best in service* for God. Therefore, we should not become complacent or stagnant. Our anticipation should not only be on *acquiring* God's best, but also on *achieving* God's best.

As chapter 23 of 1 Samuel unfolds, David had recovered from his previous low state. He was back in fellowship with God again, he was listening to God again, and God was leading him again. Nevertheless, Saul was still relentless in his personal quest to destroy David. Saul represents our satanic foe that is ever relentless in seeking our destruction. Saul resumed the activities of his favorite pastime, which was to get David.

The Treacherous Scheme

For an objective analysis of Saul's treatment of David, consideration must be given to Saul's mental state. After all, our court system makes allowances for acts of crime committed during insanity. However, Saul's actions toward David may not have been totally the result of his insanity. After all, he was doing crazy things before he went insane. That's how he got in trouble with God in the first place. That's why God rent the kingdom from his rule. His hostility toward David could be attributed more to his meanness than to his madness.

When he discovered David's new hiding place, he resumed

his hunt with the same vengeful intention as before. To increase the intensity of the search for David, he offered his men an incentive by subtle implication. He said, "*Will the son of Jesse give every one of you fields and vineyards, and make you all captains of thousands, and captains of hundreds*?"

Please note that this offer was given to his relatives the Benjamites. He shrewdly appealed to nepotism to solicit help in finding David. Perhaps the appeal was more manipulative than shrewd. It was a treacherous scheme influenced by manipulative shrewdness.

Manipulation is, of course, a common carnal behavior. Employers manipulate employees and employees manipulate employers. Husbands manipulate wives and wives manipulate husbands. Parents manipulate children and – guess what? Children manipulate parents. Sometimes one family member manipulates the entire family, and it's not necessarily the patriarch or the matriarch of the family. It can be someone far down in the pecking order of siblings who manipulates the entire family, including aunts and uncles and cousins. Manipulation in itself is a treacherous scheme.

It is enlightening to see the elements of Saul's manipulation. The elements are *greed, glory,* and *guilt*.

"*Will the son of Jesse give every one of you fields and vineyards*?" That's the first one, greed. The propensity of greed attracts manipulation. A person may use wealth to manipulate a greedy person, but a greedy person can manipulate the wealthy as well. Saul implied that he had fields and vineyards as rewards for the men who would help him catch David.

The second is *glory*. He also indicated he would give out promotions as captains of thousands, and captains of hundreds. That definitely appeals to our glory. The propensity of humanity is we can never get enough glory. We can never hear our name called enough. No one can tell us how good we are enough. We never can hear enough accolades and platitudes. Following close on the heels of greed is glory.

People who want places of position are vulnerable to this kind manipulation. People who feel as if they are on the outside of the inner circle can be targeted for this kind of manipulation.

Saul's offer was based on *prosperity* and *position*. He appealed to the fact that we never seem to be pleased with our position in life.

The third element essential for greed is *guilt*. People who can't offer possessions or positions will utilize guilt. Saul said, "*All of you have conspired against me and none of you disclosed to me that my son made a league with the son of Jesse, and there is none of you who is sorry for me.*"

This statement was purposely made to generate guilt. Who could feel sorry for an insecure, insensitive, selfish, self-serving person like Saul? Most manipulators use guilt in some form. Here Saul is sitting atop the highest seat in the land as King of Israel. He is receiving tribute money from subjugated kingdoms. He has workers in his kingdom like Doeg, who work exclusively for his welfare – and he wanted his subordinates to feel sorry for him. Saul's offer, obviously, was based on prosperity, position, and pity.

Doeg responded to Saul's manipulative challenge. This is his second appearance in Scripture. He was present when David came to Ahimelech and asked for bread. Doeg represents people who are easy targets for manipulation. He was an Edomite, which means he was not an Israelite. And Saul's inner circle was made up of Benjamites.

Outsiders often feel like they have to prove their worth so they can be accepted. They feel as if they have to buy friendship and make people like them. So Doeg eagerly spoke up. He was a ripe candidate for manipulation. He told Saul that he had seen David when he came to Ahimelech. An interesting fact is that the Bible says Doeg was there among the priests that day because he was "detained before the Lord." Doeg conveniently did not say why he was there. He voluntarily offered the information that he saw David, but did not volunteer why the priests were detaining him.

He not only said that he saw David, but he embellished the story. He lied and said Ahimelech inquired of the Lord for David. Ahimelech did no such thing. Furthermore, he intimated that Ahimelech gave David provisions. All he gave David was some dried up bread that had been removed so fresh bread could be placed before the Lord. About all that bread was good for was to make a person thirsty for more water than David had to drink.

As a result of Doeg's personally motivated information, Saul summoned all the priests from Nob to Gibeah, interrogated Ahimelech, and summarily pronounced a death sentence on him and his household. However, none of Saul's soldiers would carry out the sentence. Consequently, the king said to Doeg, "You turn and kill the priests." And Doeg killed the full compliment of priests, eighty-five in number, including the entire population of the city of Nob. However, Abiathar, one of the sons of Ahimelech escaped and fled to David.

The Tragic Sentence

Saul's sentence was upon Ahimelech *and his father's entire house*. That meant all the descendants of Eli were sentenced to death. Sons inherited the priesthood from their father.

It was, indeed, *a tragic sentence*. It was tragic in its *magnitude*. However, it was also tragic because of the *means* by which Saul arrived at the sentence. Saul had only one witness and the Law stated that at least two or three witnesses were required for capital punishment.

Nevertheless, we should not be too chagrined by what Saul did. People in church condemn others with no witnesses at all, and with no evidence either. However, when Saul gave the command to kill all the priests, no soldier moved. None of them unsheathed their sword. They remained at attention. A quote about this heinous command says, "*Never was a command by a king more barbarically given and never was a command by a king more honorably disobeyed.*" "*But the servants of the King would not lift their hand to strike the priests of the Lord.*"

So Saul gave the command to Doeg. Doeg was not a soldier. Only a soldier was supposed to do this kind of execution. What was Doeg's occupation? He was a herdsman who was dissatisfied with his position. He wanted to be a soldier. More specifically, he wanted to be one of the captains over a hundred or, better yet, over a thousand.

We should not compromise our personhood, manhood, or womanhood for any kind of glory, or for any kind of position. Notwithstanding, Doeg was more than willing to carry out the execution.

Earlier I alluded to the properties of manipulation, which are *greed, glory and guilt*. However, the purpose is to gain gratitude from the manipulator. Saul was the one who wanted the priests dead. Their deaths fed his sick psyche for wanting to get David. The sociological, psychological, and spiritual implication of Saul's act is overwhelming in significance.

The Trusting Subjects

As tragic as Saul's sentence was for the Priests and the City of Nob, nevertheless, one priest managed to escape. Abiathar, one of the sons of Ahimelech, was able to flee and he ran and told David how Saul had ordered all the priests to be killed and their families. David replied to Abiathar with these grief stricken words, "*I knew that day, when Doeg the Edomite was there, that he would surely tell Saul. I have caused the death of all the persons of your father's house.*" However, what David did not know was what Saul would do after Doeg told him he had seen him. Certainly a man of David's constitution would feel responsible for innocent deaths. A man of David's compassion would take the blame for the tragic incident, and he did.

It is a strong indication of spiritual maturity when we accept responsibility for our harmful and hurtful actions. However, it is even a stronger indication of spiritual maturity when accept responsibility for the harmful and hurtful actions of someone else. The grief that you experience from knowing what you did (even indirectly) has hurt someone can steal your joy out of your journey. It can take the sweet taste out of worship. It can drive sleep from your eyes. That's why this was a case for God. God has poignant grace for this peculiar kind of grief.

Let's consider the question: was David responsible for the deaths of all those priests? We would have to say not totally. He *was responsible* for his deception before Ahimelech. However, *he was not responsible* for the embellished lie that Doeg attached to the truth about him asking Ahimelech for bread.

Neither was David responsible for Saul's mean, treacherous, sick intent to hurt him by killing the priests. He was not responsible for that. The argument, of course, could be that if David had not gone to Ahimelech the tragedy would not have happened. Likewise, if Doeg had not lied to Saul it might not have happened. And, if Saul hadn't had such a twisted psyche and hatred for David, it definitely would not have happened. That is why it was a case for God.

God knows how to discern all that was right and all that was wrong in this case. God knows how to fairly mete out justice in a complicated case. After all, He is the judge of all the earth. And He does not need a jury to file out and deliberate on testimony and evidence. Through His omniscience He will not condemn the innocent neither will He clear the guilty.

The trusting subjects were David and Abiathar. They were both hurting when they met each other. Abiathar was hurting because of the *results* of the tragedy. David was hurting because he felt *responsible* for the tragedy. Two different kinds of painful emotions were embodied in those two men.

Yet through their different kind of pain they to interacted and bonded with each other. Their bond was solidified by the fact that they were both objects of Saul's murderous intentions. That was precisely David's assessment of their predicament. He told Abiathar, "*Stay with me; do not fear. For he who seeks my life seeks your life, but with me you shall be safe.*"

It is impossible to determine if Abiathar held any animosity toward David for the deaths of the priests and their families (including his family). If he had any animosity he had to deal with it quickly because they needed each other for survival. David needed him for *spirituality* and he needed David for *safety*. They modeled Christian fellowship. As the Body of Christ, we are not independent of each other. We have to rely on each other for service and survival.

Perhaps Abiathar was in the worst position of the two. If he blamed David for killing off his entire household he was in big trouble, because David was going to become king one day. It is very likely that they helped each other deal with their pain. Later on in the narrative it shows how they complimented each other with their leadership.

For example, the return of the Ark of the Covenant back to Jerusalem was the orchestrated leadership of these two men. They made a good team. David needed Abiathar and Abiathar also needed him. God used the union of these two men for His glory. After David became king he appointed Abiathar the High Priest.

WAITING...WATCHING... WORKING

Chapter Twelve

1 Samuel 23:1-29

When the curtain of time opens on this text David's circumstances have *changed slightly* as a fugitive. He was still a fugitive of course, but he now had the company of other fugitives. Nearly six hundred men had gravitated to him while he was hiding out in the cave of Adullam.

His circumstances had *changed significantly* by the fact that he had become the leader of these men. Through the view of hindsight we can see that God used David's fugitive days to hone his leadership and his administrative skills. It was the time when God strengthened him as a *personal servant*. Furthermore, it was also the time that God strengthened him for *public service*.

As the subject indicates it was *waiting time*. David was indeed God's choice to be the next king over Israel. The prophet Samuel had secretly anointed him at his father's house. But, the anointing did not remain a secret, even though David never boasted about it, never bragged about it, and never announced it. However, somehow it still became public knowledge that David would be the next king over Israel.

That was good news for some people, but it was bad news for others. Notwithstanding, each tick of the clock was waiting time for David. He was waiting for the time that is "God's Time" to be enthroned as the King of Israel. It's always critical to realize that God's timing may not be our timing. However, to his credit David never lifted a finger through out the nearly sixteen years of waiting to help him self to become King of Israel.

Also this was *watching time*. David had to be alert for both physical and spiritual developments. The primary physical development was the ever-increasing, relentless intention of Saul to kill him.

Saul's many attempts to kill David are not as unrelated to twenty-first century Christians as they may initially seem. To the contrary, we live in a time when there are "crazies" who stalk victims over long periods of time in a similar way as to how Saul pursued David. So David's story relates to our time, perhaps, more keenly than we may realize.

Lastly, it was a *working time*. David was certainly not idle during his fugitive days and indications are that while he was *waiting* on the Lord he was also *working* for the Lord in the sense of his preparation for being king.

The Problem

The problem confronting David and his men was the news of random recurring attacks by the Philistine soldiers on the border towns of Judah. The Philistine soldiers plundered and robbed these defenseless border towns that happened to be located near their border. And, even though he was an outcast, David still had a sense of loyalty and patriotism to his country. His position was a lot like the position of African Americans in this country. We have never been able to swim in the mainstream of American life, yet we have fought in every war that our nation has engaged in since and including the Revolutionary War.

In high school I learned about the shot heard around the world. But it was not until I was in college that I found out that shot killed a black man, Crispus Attucks, who was the first casualty of the Revolution. Without receiving rewards and recognition we have, nonetheless, served our county honorably.

David had this same peculiar privilege. He was not enjoying the benefits of his citizenship in Israel, but felt personally encroached upon by the random attacks on the defenseless cities. He commanded six hundred trained men, and it was difficult to just sit by and do nothing in response to these senseless, vicious attacks by the roving Philistine soldiers.

One of the cities subject to these attacks was Keilah. It was near David's hideout, which made the attacks even more problematic for him in two senses. One, if he and his men retaliated against the Philistines it would reveal his whereabouts to the Philistines, who were his enemy. Two, guess who else would know where he was? It would also reveal his whereabouts to Saul, who treated him as an enemy.

So the problem was twofold. To fight would put him in jeopardy with two enemies, the Philistines and Saul. His predicament is described as being "between a rock and a hard place." However, unlike in previous times when David faced dilemmas and quandaries and had made rash, rushed, thoughtless, and spur of the moment decisions, this time he prayed and consulted God first.

The Prayer

The experiences of fleeing to Nob and then to Gath had taught David to pray before he made decisions to move. They were lessons well learned. No doubt all the disastrous consequences of attempting to hide out in Gath came to his memory.

Now, however, in the face of such problems, he had learned to pray before taking any action.

And that is a good lesson for Christians to learn in every generation's time. I don't mean learning *HOW* to pray, I mean learning *TO* pray. "How to pray" refers to the *form of prayer*, but "to pray" refers to the *fact of prayer*. The fact of praying is far more important than the form of praying. The seriousness of praying is more significant than the style of praying, which is taught in the words of a hymn that I still love:

Oh what peace we often forfeit,
Oh what needless pain we bear.
All because we do not carry
EVERYTHING to God in prayer.

David had not only learned the *form of praying*, he had learned the *fact of praying*. Neither had he only learned the style of praying he had learned the *seriousness of praying*. On previous occasions, he had paid a high price for not praying first. This time his motive, first and foremost, would be the will of God. This time he intended to move in the will of God. So he prayed. His prayer was short, simple and succinct, but it was serious.

The total content of his prayer was only a few words: "*Lord shall I go and smite the Philistines*?"

Among the many lessons about praying that we should learn is that the more directly we pray, the more direct our answers from God will be. Some people don't pray directly enough. It's what I call "shotgun praying" as opposed to "single shot praying."

Pray specifically. Pinpoint your prayer.

Some one wisely said, "If you aim at nothing, you will hit it every time." David's direct prayer got a direct response. *Shall I go? And what did God say*? "*Go!*" However, the problem has never been with God's *direction*. The problem has always been with our *hesitation* after receiving God's clear direction. You have done it, I'm sure, and I've done it, I know; that is to say "no" when God has said "go."

After the *response from his Master*, David was faced with a *reaction from his men.* Here is yet another lesson to learn about praying. We must not let the *voices of men* detour us from *the voice of the Master.* The message from his men was that they were afraid just being in Judah, and that it would be more hazardous to go to Keilah to fight the Philistines. In simple terms they said to David, "Look man, it doesn't make sense to go looking for trouble. Trouble can find us right here where we are." However, the true test of a leader is not to be persuaded by the voice of the people when God has spoken plainly.

David's men spoke out of fear. There is no emotion or temptation like fear. If we were to rank grievous sins, we would have to put "fear" near the top, and close behind fear would be "unbelief" because fear gives birth to unbelief. What's more, fear can dominate faith. When we don't have enough faith, fear will take over. It is one of the main reasons Christians are often defeated.

So David prayed again and this time the Lord answered him with more emphasis and specifics than the first time. The first time God simply said, "*Go*" but this time God said, "*Arise and go.*" The second answer had a parental tone to it. It was like hearing your parents say, "Didn't I tell you to do such and such?" That's precisely the implication of God's second response to David. However, it was not only God's emphasis that gave David his confirmation; it was also the specifics of God's answer. God added more assurance than He did the first time. It was implied that he was going to give him victory when he told him to go.

God doesn't send us out to be defeated. Since when has God ordered his armies to go out and be defeated? Victory was implied when God said, "Go" the first time, but the second time the communication was more specific. This time God included some assurance and said, "*I will deliver the Philistines into your hands.*" The next words in the sequence describe the results when David followed God's instructions: "*So David and his men went to Keilah, and fought with the Philistines, and brought away their cattle, and smote them with a great slaughter. So David saved the inhabitants of Keilah.*"

The impact of those words relates to the leadership that David exhibited before his men. They were opposed to going at first, but the leadership character of David withstood their objections. A leader must follow the voice of his Savior not the voices of his subordinates.

A final lesson in prayer can be taken from this episode and it is that "God's performance will always match His promise." If God promised it, God will perform it. God's promise to David was, "*Go and I will deliver the Philistines into your hand.*" And the performance was, "*So David saved the inhabitants of Keilah.*"

There will always be direct correlation between God's promise and His *performance.* If God said that He would do it, it will come to pass.

The Predicament

As mentioned earlier the risk of helping the residents of Keilah was that Saul would discover where David and his men were located. "*It was told to Saul that David had gone to Keilah.*" This was the predicament that David anticipated. The attack on the Philistines revealed his location not only to the Philistines, but also to Saul. When Saul heard that David was in Keilah, he said, "*God has delivered him into my hand; because he is shut in by entering a town that has gates and bars.*"

If it is not puzzling to you, it is puzzling to me as to how Saul would conclude that God had delivered David into his hand. He apparently didn't remember when Samuel told him, "*I will not return with you for you have rejected the Word of the Lord, you have rejected the Word of the Lord and the Lord has rejected you from being king over Israel.*" And when Samuel turned about to walk away Saul took hold to the skirt of his mantle and tore it in his attempt to restrain Samuel from leaving.

Now were Samuel's words clear or not? How could Saul miss the meaning of Samuel's pronouncement that God had rejected him as king of Israel?

The fact is that he did not miss the meaning; he ignored it. He refused it. There is the viewpoint that suggests Saul's behavior could be attributed to the fact that he had "lost his salvation." It is concluded that his behavior flowed out of an unconscious unsaved soul. This viewpoint will be addressed more completely later in another place in the narrative. The truth is that a person does not have to be unsaved to adamantly refuse the will of God. A person does not have to be unsaved to obstinately reject the Word of God. That was the case with Saul.

The question that could be asked is: why didn't God simply remove Saul from his antagonistic place in David's life? After all, God could just snap His fingers and Saul would have been off the throne and David would have been on the throne in his place. God instead used Saul's obstinacy to strengthen David's obedience. In a general sense God uses negative encounter and experiences for positive results.

However, the predicament that David found himself in was like a "Catch 22." There was no move he could make except one. Guess what his only move was: prayer.

And David prayed again. He was three for three with his prayers. He prayed for deliverance from Gath, prayed for God's direction in defending the people of Kielah, and prayed about the predicament that he suddenly found himself in.

Here is a word for people who say they can't pray. When enough trouble comes they will pray, and pray earnestly and fervently. This is the content of David's prayer: "*Oh Lord God of Israel, your servant has certainly heard that Saul seeks to come down here.*"

David had heard that Saul was on his way to his stronghold, and from that we can determine that both David and Saul had spies checking on the other. David was no one's fool. In the prayer he inquired, "*Will the man of Keilah deliver me up into his hands? Will Saul come down as your servant has heard? O Lord God of Israel, I beseech you, tell your servant.*" And the Lord said, "*He will come down.*"

However, God had only responded to part of David's prayer. So David repeated a portion of his prayer and inquired again,

"*Will the men of Keilah deliver me and my men into the hand of Saul?*" And the Lord said, "*They will deliver you up.*"

Here is another lesson for us from the life of David. It is possible, after you have befriended someone, after you were available for someone, after someone needed you and you were there, it's possible for that person to turn on you. When the dust of controversy has settled, it's possible for people whom you have helped to "deliver you up."

It is possible for a man to have loved his wife for many years, as Christ loved the church, but when the tide of life was low she gave him up. It's possible for a woman to honor a man in love and submission, but when the ducks were all lined up in a row, he gave her up. The friend whom you took to your bosom, and who took you to his bosom, the friend who you opened your life to, and who opened his life to you, is no longer was your friend when the clouds of innuendo and suspicion began to gather over you. He gives you up. Lord have mercy, it can happen to you in a twenty-four hour period. The betrayal of David by the people of Keilah is the risk factor for the help we feel constrained to give.

This just proves that there is no relationship, no friendship, and no fellowship that is as constant and consistent as our relationship with the Lord. Friends come and go. However, the old hymn was right:

There is not a friend like the lowly Jesus.
No not one. No not one
No one like Him is so high and holy
No not one, no not one.
And none like him who's so meek and lowly
No not one, no not one.

Furthermore, the risk of betrayal extends past *friends* and includes *family*. This doesn't mean that we are not supposed to have special love, affection and attention for our family, but it simply means *anyone, anywhere, anytime,* about *anything*, and sometimes about nothing, can give you up.

This incident not only teaches us about the *reality* of betrayal, but also what the *response* should be. After the Lord revealed to David the intention to betray him, *he left*. Don't miss that. "*Then David and his men who were about six hundred in number arose and departed out of Keilah, and went wherever they could go.*"

What is the proper response when somebody has betrayed you or given you up? *Move on*! That's precisely what David did. He did not reveal to them that he knew their intentions to betray him. Neither did he exact any punishment on them. He simply left. David models the right response for us. Move on with your life and do not look back. Set your compass and direct your life toward the bright future on your horizon.

"*And David abode in the wilderness in strongholds, and remained in a mountain in the wilderness of Ziph. And Saul sought him every day, but God delivered him not into his hand.*"

How often did Saul search for David? *Every day!* Now be sure to observe this: the undetected movement of more than six hundred men in a wilderness could only be the result of the miraculous hand of God. Imagine the environmental impact of more than six hundred men in a wilderness. It doesn't matter which forest you name: Amazon, Redwoods, Yellowstone, Yosemite – any forest, just name it. Six hundred men in any forest would leave a horrendous environmental mess.

Think about it, six hundred men on the move would be easy to track. Consider the amount of body waste six hundred men could produce. It doesn't matter what the amount of natural resources were in the forest. The amount of foliage wouldn't matter. Six hundred men would leave all kinds of tracks and trails as to their whereabouts. My goodness, Ray Charles and Stevie Wonder could have found them. But the Bible says, "*Saul sought him every day, but God delivered him not into to his hand.*"

Six hundred men were undetected in the wilderness of Ziph; that's incredible. More specifically, it's miraculous. The explanation for their not being detected is in the meaning of the Hebrew word, *halak*. It has nearly seventy definitions. It is the word that is translated to mean they "*went where they could go.*"

It's an interesting translation to English. They didn't go where they *would* go, but went where they *could* go. However, one of the definitions for *halak* is to disappear. *David and his six hundred men went into the forest and disappeared.* And they went into strongholds *and disappeared*, and on a mountain *and disappeared.* That is why Saul couldn't find them. And it may be the experience behind David's words in Psalm 91: "*He will cover you with His feathers and under His wing shall you trust.*"

The predicament wasn't only that the people of Kielah were going to betray him; it was replicated when David arrived in Ziph. The Ziphites came to Saul and said, "*David hides himself with us in strongholds in the forest. Come down and our part shall be to deliver him into the king's hand.*"

Long story short, Saul came again with his army and once again God protected David and his men. "*And Saul went on this side of the mountain, and David and his men went on that side of the mountain.*"

The other times when Saul came to capture David, he didn't get close. That means God protected David and his men at a distance while they were in the wilderness, and God protected them at close range on the side of the mountain.

"*Saul and his men compassed David and his men round about to take them.*" In simple terms, David and his men played peek-a-boo on the side of the mountain with Saul and his army.

"*Then there came a messenger to Saul, saying, 'Make haste and come for the Philistines have invaded the land.' So Saul returned from pursuing after David and went after the Philistines.*"

This shows that God can protect us directly or indirectly. It shows that God can use human events for our protection. He doesn't have to perform a miracle to protect us. He can just use human events or natural occurrences in life for our good.

God can work the layoff from a job for our good. He can work through our illness, or that of a loved one. God can work in a divorce. God can work in a bankruptcy. God can work through both natural and unnatural occurrences.

The Philistines weren't fools. While Saul was focusing all his energy and time on attempting to capture David and his men, they launched an offensive against Israel. This caused Saul to abandon his military operation to get David and give his attention to the safety of his homeland.

The Protection

David's deliverance from Gath proved that God was his protector. And, the deliverance from the wilderness of Ziph was more proof that God was his protector. Lest we forget, David was on the comeback from a tragic faith lapse. He had never been lower than he was when he lied to the priest, and then attempted to take refuge the enemy's camp.

That wasn't just a faith lapse; it was plain dumbness. Nevertheless, here he was on sound footing again. He was back in fellowship with God.

We not only learn about David from a study of his life, we also learn about God. We can see love, grace, mercy, and long suffering in the maturing process of God's servant, David. This is the same love, grace, mercy, and long suffering that we receive in our maturing process to being a servant of God.

God used betrayal as a faith building block for David. Betrayal is one of the most difficult offenses for us to survive – and David was given two doses of human betrayal. God used the fickleness of human behavior to make sure David knew he could trust Him to be his protector and his provider.

Furthermore, sandwiched between these betrayals by the people of Keilah and the people of Ziph was the reappearance of Jonathan to encourage and reassure him. This was good support and symbolizes our need Christian fellowship. It is good evidence as to why we need deep roots of Christian fellowship. Often what we need to continue through a difficult period can come through another brother or sister in the Lord. Unfortunately, this was the last time David saw Jonathan alive.

The ultimate meaning behind this narrative is that God would be and was David's protector. God really turned on a display of His power for David in this story. God also showed David His vitality by protecting him from a distance, and showed David His versatility by protecting him at close range.

Finally God showed David His variety by protecting through a common occurrence. The lesson for David and for us is that God can protect secretly or openly. He can do it visibly invisibly. Actually, God can protect anyway you want it. This chapter of David's life closed with these words: "*And David went up from there and dwelt in the strongholds of Engedi.*"

DAVID AT ENGEDI

Chapter Thirteen

1 Samuel 24: 1-22

You may find it interesting, as I did, to discover that David moved approximately sixteen times to escape the vengeful, relentless pursuit of King Saul. This represents a change of location for each of his fugitive years. Nevertheless, David learned *new lessons* at each *new location*. Furthermore, the new lessons sharpened, shaped, and strengthened his spiritual maturity. From forest to cave, from cave to wildernesses, from wilderness to mountaintop, there were new lessons for David to learn.

And his move to the cave at Engedi was no exception.

The entire sixteen fugitive years were like graduate level preparation for *who he would be* and *for what he would do* as the next king of Israel. The applications of his movements provide insights that can be used for whatever experience we go through is our preparation for the next level of living.

David's stay at Engedi takes us deeper into the life and history of this great Bible character. Up until now we have only looked at a small portion of his life, and we have seen that David had weak moments as well as strong moments. He had his worst moments and he had his best moments.

That, perhaps, is the reason David is the favorite Old Testament personality for many Christians, because we can so easily identify with him. He is so much like us. His fleshly humanity was transparent, sometimes shamefully transparent, and sometimes even disgustingly transparent. However, at Engedi he was at his best.

The exceptions for David were the times when he was at his worst, not when he was at his best. Opposite to David is Saul, the exceptions for him being when he was at his best. At Engedi David is the example for every serious disciple of the Lord, but not Saul. Our worst behavior should be the exception, though for some people that may not be true. For some people their best is the exception and their worst is the norm. Here at Engedi David models for us the best behavior of a servant of God.

The Persecution Resumed

In the previous chronicle of David's life, God miraculously protected him and his six hundred men from the relentless pursuit of King Saul. They fled into a forest and "*Saul sought him everyday, but God delivered him not into his hand.*" It takes very little imagination to see that it was a lot more difficult for David to hide with six hundred men than it would have been for him to hide when he was alone and on the run.

But, it was not more difficult for God.

It was no more difficult for God to hide him and six hundred men than it was to hide David by himself. Nevertheless, David still needed God's protection because the hunt for him was still on.

"*Then Saul took three thousand chosen men of Israel, and went to seek David.*" That simply means Saul resumed pursuit. Saul was a sick, insecure, schizophrenic psychopath with an insatiable hatred for David. He represents the degree to which hate and revenge can motivate us.

Everyone has been motivated at one time or another to "get" someone. All of us have had the notion at one time or another to take revenge on someone. We have all done it, or at least wanted to do it. We've said, "I ought to get him" or "I ought to fix her," but we severed the thought and went on about our business.

The primary certainty about Saul's relentless effort to capture or kill David is the ultimate depth to which revenge will lead a person. Furthermore, it is a misuse of energy to stalk someone for your own personal revenge. It is a waste of time to stake someone out for destruction. A wise admonishment is to *let it go.* It's not worth it. It's not worth getting out of your bed in the wee hours of the morning and driving all over town trying to find out where your guy is.

There are too many men in the world!

It's a waste of energy to go and hide out in the bushes to watch and see who's coming in and going out of your lady's residence, and then to have the water sprinklers goes off on you while you're there in the bushes. It's not worth getting wet when the water sprinklers go off at three-thirty in the morning.

There are too many women out there man!

The best admonishment is to *give it up.* Life is too short to misuse time and energy like that.

Look at the energy and the man-hours Saul expended trying to catch David. It became blatantly ridiculous. This time he had three thousand *chosen men* — the best of Israel's army with him in an effort to take one man. With those three thousand men he should have been securing his nation's borders to make them safe. He could even have engaged in a military buildup as a show of strength to the Philistines. After all, the best defense is a good offense. That was proved during the Reagan administration. It's how we won the Cold War. The point is that Saul's time and effort could have been much better directed toward more profitable and meaningful matters of national concern.

The Peculiar Restraint

While on his vindictive quest, Saul was beset by the normal physiological urge and the biological function that connects all of us to our mortality; which was to relieve himself. "*And Saul went into the cave to cover his feet.*" That phrase "**to cover his feet**" is a euphemism. A euphemism is when the Bible translators used a less harsh word, or less graphic word, for a description of an act or an occurrence. Even a king was given absolute privacy to go to the toilet.

However, unknown to King Saul, he chose the cave where David and his men were hiding. They had pressed themselves against the walls of the cave to avoid detection. This was, obviously, the opportunity for David to be rid of King Saul once and for all – considering the fact that Saul was in the right position and about as defenseless as a person could be.

Nevertheless, it was not an opportunity for David. It may, perhaps, have been someone else's opportunity, but not David's. His men pressured him and urged him to take matters into his own hands. They were whispering, of course, and gesturing with their hands for David to seize the opportunity, thinking that God had providentially arranged this occasion for him. In fact, they said to David, "*This is the day that the Lord told you, 'Behold I will deliver your enemy into your hand, that you may do to him as it shall seem good unto you.'*"

David, however, exhibited what I am calling *peculiar restraint*. But it is only peculiar to people who see through non-spiritual eyes. It is only peculiar for people who do not have spiritual vision. It is, on the other hand, also peculiar to people of God, yet we are somewhat familiar with this kind of restraint. This is the kind of behavior we have been instructed by the Lord to display all the time. Consequently, David's restraint is supposed to be expected, not unexpected, behavior to the people of God.

With this restraint David epitomized the higher dimension of Godly behavior. David was way ahead of his class. If you compare his life to a race, he was far ahead of the pack with this display of restraint. What David did hadn't even come into vogue until the Lord Jesus came preaching and teaching about turning the other cheek and going another mile.

David lived during the time when it was "*eye for an eye, tooth for tooth, hand for hand, foot for foot, burning for burning, wound for wound, stripe for stripe.*" His behavior toward Saul in this cave was far above the standard of his day.

Jesus replaced the old standard with a new standard. We call it the Sermon on the Mount. Jesus said, "*You have heard it said, 'You shall love your neighbor, and hate your enemy;' but I say love your enemies, bless them that curse you, do good to them that hate you, and pray for them who despitefully use you and persecute you.*"

My goodness, David was practicing a behavior that hadn't been articulated yet.

Previously, David was tested by a twofold betrayal and he passed the test. The conclusion was that a betrayal is one of the most difficult experiences to deal with and overcome. But David handled his betrayals with flying colors.

Notwithstanding, the ability to refuse the opportunity for revenge is equal to the experience of betrayal. Too few Christians can do that. We have the complete revealed Word of God at our disposal, but we can't do it. We have the indwelling ministry of the Holy Spirit, and we still can't overcome the motivation for revenge.

David's men urged him on.

It's wise to be careful of who we take advice from when we have the opportunity for revenge. We are vulnerable to the temptation of revenge. Think about it, a clear shot of revenge is a whole lot of temptation. So please be careful who you listen to when you have the opportunity for revenge. Watch out for the person who will say, "If I were you, I wouldn't take that," or "If it was me, I would do this or that."

Your response should be, "Perhaps, but you're not me."

That's the big difference. Maybe the person trying to give you advice hasn't been touched by God the way you have. Maybe the person giving you his or her advice hasn't been walking as close to God as you have.

As David observed Saul in his defenseless position, it's rather certain that he may have thought about God's promise that he would be the next King of Israel. Recent occurrences had, of course, made that promise appear to be ever more remote. And the more distant an opportunity is, the stronger the temptation will be for us to want to help it come to fruition. The more remote God's promises appear, the harder it is for us not to interfere.

We say to God, "I need my blessing by Thursday at four o'clock. If you don't come through for me by Thursday at four o'clock, I'm going to have to use my MasterCard. I can't wait any longer."

It's a strong temptation. David was a long stretch from becoming king. The hint of the text is that for a slight moment, perhaps, David yielded to the urgings of his men and was tempted to kill Saul. He snatched his knife out of its sheath and started in the direction of Saul, but by the time he got there his desire and motivation has waned and all he did was cut off a little piece of the King's royal robe – and just doing hurt him to his heart.

His *hand* couldn't do what his *heart* wouldn't let it do. We must not forget the kind of heart David had. He was a man after God's own heart. That means his heart was like God's heart. That's why he was embarrassed for the little disrespect he had shown Saul by cutting off a piece of his garment.

I would like to have seen the look of surprise on his men's faces when he explained why he didn't kill the King. Here is his explanation: "*The Lord forbid that I should do this to my master, to stretch forth my hand against him, since he is the Lord's anointed.*"

David's explanation takes me back to some of my boyhood scenes in my father's house. My father had a rather heavy hand when it came to corporal discipline.

"A.J. did not play!"

I never debated the fact that I didn't deserve the licking. Actually, it didn't make any difference if I was guilty or not. There was no redress process in Albert Winters' house. So I would complain to my mother that the punishment didn't match the crime, and she would inevitably say, "That's your Daddy."

That's all the response I got.

I would attempt to show her my bruises to get her sympathy, but I still got the same response: "He's your daddy." That's the response I received every time. And, it's the same response David gave to his men: "*He's the King*."

It didn't matter that Saul had been trying to kill him *he was still the King*. It didn't matter that Saul had made him a fugitive, or had taken his wife and given her to another man, or that he had maligned David's character, *he was still the King*. My goodness, it brings tears to my eyes to see that David had such a deep capacity of love and respect for Saul when he, obviously, didn't love and respect him in return.

So David displayed a *peculiar restraint*. He refused to take Saul's life, but not because of fear. He restrained himself, but not because he lost his nerve. It was because he perceived Saul as the Lord's anointed. The Holy Spirit showed a deeper meaning of this *peculiar restraint* and that is, it was not only who Saul was that caused David to restrain himself, it was also who David was that caused this restraint. It wasn't really about Saul; it was more so about David.

Wait! there is more peculiar behavior by David. David followed Saul right out of that cave, out into the open, and into public view in front of all of Saul's soldiers and his own mighty men. There he challenged Saul in a civil confrontation.

That is the kind of confrontation we are supposed to be involved in. He asked Saul, "*Why do you listen to people who are saying that I want to do you harm*."

David did not only suffer from the fact that Saul was trying to kill him, he also suffered from the maligning of his character and his good name. The truth is that Saul, in his psychopathic schizophrenia, did not need anyone to tell him anything bad about David. He could conjure up enough negative perceptions about David without the help of anyone.

Then David showed him the evidence; the piece of his garment that he had cut off while he was *covering his feet* in the cave. Once again David was functioning at a high level of spiritual maturity. He held up the piece of cloth, the evidence that he could have taken Saul's life if he had wanted to.

Dr. Martin Luther King, Jr. made this classic and classy statement: "*Don't ever let anyone who hates you drag you so low that you start hating them in return.*"

David continued his statement with these words: "*You can see that the Lord delivered you today into my hand in the cave; my own men urged me to kill you, but I spared you because you are the Lord's anointed. See the skirt of your robe in my hand that I cut off when I could have killed you. There is neither evil nor transgression in me toward you and yet you hunt my soul to take it. The Lord judge between you and me, but my hand shall not be upon you.*"

This incident did, indeed, bring out the best behavior in David.

The Partial Repentance

"*When David ceased speaking, Saul lifted up his voice and wept,*" but it was only partial repentance. It was partial, indicating that it was superficial repentance. And Saul said to David, "*You are more righteous than me. You rewarded me well and I have rewarded you evil. You showed me kindness today, for as much as when the Lord delivered me into your hand you did not kill me. If a man finds his enemy, will he let him go away well? I know you will surely be the king and that your kingdom will be established.*"

These were nice words, but they were only *partial repentance*. And they were selfish words as well. Saul pleaded, "*When you do become king, spare my family line.*" In that day, when a new king came to the throne it was the custom for him to kill everyone in the family line of the previous king. Saul begged for his family to be spared. And David swore to him that he would spare his family.

However, what Saul promised David was not important; it's what David promised Saul that was important. What Saul said could not be taken seriously, but what David said could. So help me, I'm trying to live at the level that David displayed in this story. I know what it's like to hear unkind comments about me, and sometimes I know who has made those unkind comments. But I want to live at a mature level of development so that when I am lied about I won't lie about the other person in return. Irrespective of who may rejoice in my failure, I won't rejoice in his or her failure. That's a level of living worth aiming for – and, thanks to David, we know it is attainable.

The Precautious Reality

David's precaution is seen by the fact that he didn't return with Saul to his residence in the king's palace. "*Saul went home, but David and his men went up into the stronghold.*" That was his precautious reality. David apparently intuitively knew that Saul wasn't going to stay home. He had heard similar promises from Saul.

It reminds me of a story about a freezing snake that I heard when a boy. The scene of this story took place in Louisiana where snakes talk. It goes like this: One day a man was walking along a country road on a cold and wintry morning, and it was snowing like crazy. He noticed a snake by the side of the road that was nearly frozen to death. The snake had been trying to get someone to help him, but without success. He also asked this guy for help, telling the man that in his nearly frozen condition he wouldn't be able to make it back to his den where he could warm himself. He asked the man if he would put him inside his coat and warm him up, and then he would go on his way to his den. The man was skeptical and told the snake, "If I put you inside my coat, you may bite me."

But the snake assured the man that he wouldn't bite him. So

the man picked up the snake, put him inside his coat, and continued to walk down the road. Sure enough, when the snake got warm he crawled up and position himself so he could look the man in the face and said, "I ought to bite you."

The man said, "You can't bite me because you promised that if I helped you get warm, you wouldn't bite me."

But the snake said, "When I made you that promise I was still a snake."

I have never forgotten that story because it represents what David knew about Saul. That's why David went back to his stronghold. No matter what Saul said, he was still a snake.

Just as David suspected, it wasn't long before Saul was back on his trail again. These words were recorded a short time after Saul left David at Engedi: "*Then Saul arose and went down to the wilderness of Ziph, having three thousand chosen men of Israel with him to seek David.*"

Don't think for a moment that precaution does not have its place. The first time someone acts up on you, you can say it was an accident. The second time the person acts up on you, you can call it a coincidence. But the third time, and all the times thereafter, you should take some precautions so the person won't get close enough to hurt you again.

Being a *Christian* doesn't mean you shouldn't be *cautious*. Grandma used to say, "When a dog bites you, you feed it with a long handled spoon." You may still have to interact with the person, but do it at a safe distance. Be *courteous*, but be *cautious*. Be *civil*, but don't be *crazy*. Being a Christian doesn't mean you have to be dumb.

I'm sure you agree that this is an impressive and impacting story. And it's commendable to read about how David reacted to the mistreatment of Saul. It's fine to applaud David for his restraint toward Saul. However, there should be more than *appreciation* for David's example in this narrative; there should also be *application*.

What do we take with us on our life journey from this narrative? We need a response to the question: what will be your reaction when you have been dealt with unjustly? What will you do when someone has taken advantage of you? You don't have to go "packing" for someone. There is a better response than revenge.

Nevertheless, as good as David's example is, it's not the best example. It's good all right, but it's not the best. The best example does not come from David, but comes from the Son of David. What David did in a cave is not the best, but what Jesus did on the cross is the best. The Bible says, "*Being reviled, He reviled not again.*"

David did not have rivets in his feet when he restrained himself. He didn't have nails in his hands. And he wasn't hanging from a cross when he restrained himself from revenge. No, the best example of forgiveness is the Son of David. While he was dying He said, "*Father forgive them for they know not what they do.*" The Son of David gives us the ultimate example of forgiveness and restraint from revenge.

SAUL AT ENDOR

Chapter Fourteen

1 Samuel 28: 3-20

The comparison of *David at Engedi* to *Saul at Endor* speaks volumes of spiritual inspiration. The contrast is glaringly opposite. What David did at Engedi was in God's will. What Saul did at Endor was out of God's will. What David did at Engedi was spiritual. What Saul did at Endor was satanic. What David did at Engedi was right, but what Saul did at Endor was wrong.

It's interesting to note that the actions of both men took place in caves. The two caves represent the similarity of our common opportunity to choose to do good or evil. However, it is not really the similarity of the caves that is evocative; it is the dissimilarity of the persons in the cave.

For example, all days are the same. Each day consists of a twenty-four hour period, but what makes the differences in a day are the choices that are made in the day. Furthermore, all people are essentially the same, but the major difference in people is the Godly endowment we nurture and develop. The Godly qualities in our character make us distinctive.

Consequently, it appears that the Holy Spirit would have us examine by comparison the life of David and Saul as they were brought into parallel by time. In the comparison there are similarities. We see shameful behavior in both men. We also see failures and weakness in them, but the difference between them is a single distinction, which is their personal relationship with God.

David had a deeper personal relationship with God than did Saul. The critical truth is that Saul never repented for the initial sin that caused God to take the kingdom from him and give it to David. There is never an incident in the Bible where Saul called all Israel to prayer.

Saul wrote no psalms. He could have repented and lived in quiet solitude. He could have lived in peace with God. Even though he had fallen, he still could have been forgiven.

When God forgives us we receive more than mere forgiveness. Not only does God forgive us, He *releases* us. Not only does God release us, He restores us. Not only does God *release* and *restore*, He *refreshes* us. And God not only *releases, restores* and *refreshes* us He *restarts* us.

Saul could have received the refreshing ministry of the Holy Spirit with a simple and sincere confession to God. The sad fact is, however, that Saul rebelled against God and lived his life in total rebellion to the end of his days.

The background to the events of this chapter is announced in three words: "*Samuel was dead.*" The death of Samuel provided the Philistines an opportunity and the courage to launch an all-out offensive against Israel. They had never come at Israel with such frontal aggression before, and their increased hostility was because Samuel was dead.

Saul at Endor

A vital part of any military strategy is to capitalize on the enemy's weaknesses, and the Philistines did precisely that. Make no mistake about it, the death of Samuel weakened Israel spiritually as well as militarily. They were more vulnerable than before because Samuel was dead. And, since he was dead, the Philistines felt that their chances for victory were better because there was no prophet to give Israel counsel from God.

Consequently, another battle was staged when, "*The Philistines gathered at Shunem and the Israelites gathered at Gilboa.*" Saul's reaction at the sight of the Philistine army was deplorable. "*When Saul saw the host of the Philistines, he was afraid and his heart greatly trembled.*"

The Perverted Attempt

Saul made a perverted attempt to inquire of the Lord about this battle. However, "*When Saul inquired of the Lord, the Lord answered him not.*" No detailed elaboration is needed to understand the tragedy in these words. I don't have to build a big case about the position God's refusal to answer put Saul in. God did not hear him anymore. God did not answer him, "*neither by dreams, nor by Urim nor by prophets.*"

In Bible times God often used dreams to communicate with His people, more so then than now. Nowadays most of our dreams don't mean anything. However, before there was a complete Canon of the Bible, God often used dreams to communicate with His people – but Saul couldn't even have a dream about God.

God also did not speak to him by Urim. Urim were stones that were embedded in the vests of the priests. These stones gave off a certain color glint in reflection from the sun, and it was thought that various shades of colors stood for communications from God. It was common for Urim stones to be carried in pouches for convenient reference to get direction from God, but the accuracy of the colors was more subject to chance than anything. They were actually used in much the say way as lucky charms are used.

The use of the Urim stones was done in much the same way that some Christians now utilize prayer for direction from God. They say to God, "Lord, if the sun is shining and it does not rain tomorrow, let that mean that I can drive to Los Angeles." However, the chance of the sun shining tomorrow in Southern California is usually very likely. That is not an effective, or proper, use of prayer.

An interesting fact for observation is that Urim stones were forbidden after David came to the throne. The implication is that he knew a more spiritual and accurate way to acquire direction from God. Furthermore, it marks the distinction in the spiritual quality of Saul's leadership and David's. The effectiveness of leadership is in spiritual quality of the leader. It's tragic that churches don't recognize and realize that simple truth.

Last, God did not answer Saul by prophets. No prophets brought him a word from the Lord. This is not an unfair option by God, and neither is it an unusual option by God. We find the explanation in Isaiah 59:1-3: "*Behold, the Lord's hand is not shortened that it cannot save.*" That simply means God has not lost any of His power. The Scripture passage continues with, "*neither His ear heavy that He cannot hear.*"

There is nothing wrong with God's hearing. He has no hearing deficiency. The reason He doesn't answer is, "*your iniquities have separated between you and your God, and your sins have hid His face from you that He will not hear.*"

David wrote in Psalm 51: "*If I hide iniquity in my heart, the Lord will not hear my prayer.*" The distressing reality is that when a child of God chooses to live in utter rebellion against God, God may choose to not hear when the person prays. Saul's mistake was in inquiring about *deliverance* and *safety* when he should have been praying about his *defilement* from sin.

As a matter of fact, Saul never confessed and repented for his initial sin that caused God to take the kingdom from him. He continued his life in disobedience to God. He relentlessly and consistently sought the life of an innocent man. On one occasion he even attempted to spear his own son. On another tragic day he ordered the slaughter of all the priests including their wives, children, and grandchildren. His intention was to wipe out all the priests in Israel, but one of them was able to escape and joined David in hiding. And Saul never asked God to forgive him for that barbaric and heinous act.

Saul's occult dabbling is a sullied graphic example of the low spiritual state to which a person may sink from his or her fellowship with God. The fact is that spiritual fellowship with God cannot be put on automatic pilot. It cannot be managed by remote control. It has to be nurtured day by day, week by week, and year in and year out. The lyrics of the old song are: "*I cannot live in sin and feel a Savior's love.*"

Many Christians are knowingly (some unknowingly) walking down the path of rebellion and away from God. The decline starts out with a few *initial steps*, then it turns to *gradual steps* that lead to *perpetual steps*. Saul did not get to this state overnight; it took him sixteen years. That is the same number of years he chased David. It's also the same number of years God gave him opportunity to repent and return to fellowship again.

Many people today are unknowingly walking down the road of rebellion away from God. The Christian who does not read the Bible daily, pray daily, and worship regularly is at great risk of descending past the point of no return. If you are withholding forgiveness from someone, you are at great risk. And, if you have offended someone and haven't asked to be forgiven, you are at great risk. It doesn't take much to start the downward journey away from God. Just think what had happened to the humble, shy, well-mannered son of Kish.

Saul's *perverted attempt* to get direction for his life occurred when he no longer heard from God and decided to make an alternative choice to go to a witch in a cave at Endor. Among all the restricted commands God gave to Moses for His people was the command to avoid any kind of association with witchcraft. The commands are in Leviticus and they are repeated again in

Deuteronomy. The common old King James Version description of persons who promoted or practiced witchcraft was "*people with familiar spirits.*" They are also known as *mediums.*

Understand that the kind of witch Saul needed was not a regular, every day, run-of-the-mill witch, if there is such a thing as a regular witch. He didn't need a witch who could tell him where to find some money, or who could tell him whether he would get his wife back after she ran away, or the meaning of a dream. He needed another kind of witch. He needed a witch who specialized in *necromancy.*

This is the kind of witch who can, supposedly, put a person in touch with the departed spirit. The hookup was feigned through deception, trickery, and illusion. It's a disgusting, distasteful, demonic activity in which Christians should never be involved. There are witches today who claim they can put people in touch with spirits of the dead.

Some Christians unknowingly trifle with witchcraft by having their palm read, by going to a fortune teller, by reading their horoscope, by inquiring about a person's zodiac sign, by wearing a zodiac medallion to indicate their sign, and by calling a phone number for a psychic reading. All of the aforementioned is a form of witchcraft.

To make contact with the witch, Saul had to dress in disguise and slip away under the cover of the blackness of the night. What a horrific scene that was, the King of Israel, the man appointed by God to rule over the people of God, in search of a witch to get direction for his life. However, as horrific as it was on the one hand, it had to be somewhat humorous on the other.

God has a sense of humor and it comes through loud and clear in this incident. The humorous point about Saul's quest to contact a witch was: if witches could really "divine" direction and give distinctions to people, she would have known it he was Saul no matter what kind of disguise he wore. A genuine gift of discernment cannot be fooled or foiled. If you put on a red wig today and a blonde wig tomorrow, you wouldn't confuse God.

But, this witch was fooled by Saul's disguise. A modern parallel to this incident could be the arrest of a certain famous recording artist in an airport for possession of marijuana. She is, allegedly, an ardent proponent of the psychic abilities of Miss Cleo. Well, if Miss Cleo really had psychic abilities, wouldn't she have warned her main supporter about her impending arrest? However, as revealed later, Miss Cleo has been exposed as a fraudulent phony. She even spoke with a Caribbean accent to imply she was from one of the Islands. I give her credit for, perhaps, being from Long Island, but as it turned out she wasn't from any island at all. She was born in Watts, California!

Anyway, Saul came into the cave to see the witch and she went through her usual line of security questions for her own safety. She had to be careful and cautious because Saul had outlawed witches and witchcraft when he was in fellowship with God. She spoke specifically to the disguised King and said, "*You know Saul has cut off the mediums and the spiritists from the land.*" Saul swore to her by the LORD that no harm would come to her. So we can see that Saul had strayed far from the path of righteousness that he once walked. But, he did not reach this low, wretched state overnight. His straying steps were in a gradual process of decline over a low period of time.

The Pretended Action

Feeling she was safe to ply her trade, the witch asked him whom he wanted to see and he said, "*Bring up Samuel for me.*" The *pretended action* of mediums was to arrange an apparition with a demon who would take the form of the departed person that the client wanted to see. The inspired words of the Apostle Paul shines illuminating light this *pretended action* to raise up the spirit of Samuel: "*For such are false apostles, deceitful workers,* **transforming themselves** *into apostles of Christ. And no wonder! For Satan himself* **transforms himself** *into an angel of light.*"

By the same satanic and demonic powers that can imitate angels, these demons can transform themselves to look like a departed person. Once again, it's pretended action. Another bit of humor appears in this narrative. It says, "*When the woman saw Samuel she cried out with a loud voice.*"

The Hebrew word for "saw" is "raah." It means to see plainly. When she saw Samuel "*she cried out with a loud voice.*" Don't miss that! When Saul came in to the cave she asked him "*Whom do you want me to bring up for you.*" And he said, "*Bring up Samuel for me.*"

She came with her *pretended action* and went into her séance – *hocus pocus, abracadabra, and open sesame* – and did something that looked like an Indian war dance. But, when Samuel actually showed up, "*she cried out with a loud voice*!"

Her response is written in the poetic style of the King James Version, but today we wouldn't say she *cried out*. We would say she *screamed*. She *shrieked*. She *hollered*. And, she turned over her boiling pot of witches' brew.

Why did she scream? Why did she become hysterical when she saw Samuel? Why was she screaming and running around and bumping into the walls of the cave when she saw him? Isn't he who she got paid to bring up?

The agreement, after all, was for her to bring Samuel back. Why then when she saw him did she get scared? And then why did she have the nerve to ask, "*Why have you deceived me? You are Saul.*" Keep in mind, she was going to deceive him, but was deceived herself.

The truth is that she didn't bring Samuel up. No witch, nowhere, no time, can bring someone up. In olden times or modern times, no witch has the power to bring up the spirits of dead.

Furthermore, it conflicts and confuses the truth to insist that Samuel was an apparition. Why did she holler so loud when she saw him coming up? It only leaves one option: it was really Samuel, and it was God who brought him up.

A question for consideration is: was there any other time in the Bible when God did that? The answer is yes. How many times did God do it? There was only one other time. When did God do it? It was when Jesus took Peter, James and John and went up on a mountain and was transfigured before them.

The Bible says, "*There appeared unto them Moses and Elijah.*" Notice this: Moses and Elijah *appeared* unto them but they only *spoke* to Jesus. On the other hand, Samuel *appeared* unto the *witch*, but he *spoke* only to *Saul*. Nevertheless, in neither case, in the cave at Endor or on the Mountain of Transfiguration, were these resurrections from the dead? Jesus performed resurrections almost routinely. However, Samuel, Moses and Elijah were appearances by people who were still dead.

So who brought Samuel up? God did. This was beyond the ability of any satanic power. People are foolish to pay money to anyone to put them in touch with someone who is dead. Only God can do that and He only did it twice – once in the Old Testament and once in the New Testament. This witch was scared out of her wits. Saul, who was apparently shocked by her response asked, "*What did you see?*" And she said, "*I saw a spirit ascending up out of the earth.*" Well, wasn't that what she was supposed to see? Wasn't that the product of her profession? Wasn't that what she was paid to do.

The Prophet's Announcement

Some people insist that this wasn't Samuel, that it was an apparition. Nevertheless, the narrative states that Saul "*perceived that it was Samuel.*" The Hebrew word that is translated "**perceive**" is "*dada*" and it means to *understand clearly*. The message given lends credence to the fact that it was Samuel. The narrative prefaced the announcement with these words, "*and Samuel said.*"

This is a first-person expression by the writer of this text that was under the inspiration of the Holy Spirit. We can tell it was Samuel by the content of the announcement. No demon apparition could have made this announcement. Samuel asked: "*Why have you disturbed me by bringing me up?*" Remember, Samuel had been in the *Land of Unclouded Days*. He had been sitting at the table of Abraham, Isaac and Jacob. So it doesn't sound like he was too enthused about being brought up. Saul's complaint and response was: "*I am deeply distressed; for the Philistines make war against me, and God has departed from me and does not answer me anymore, neither by prophets nor by dreams. Therefore, I have called you that you may reveal to me what I should do.*"

Samuel then said to Saul: "*So why do you ask me, seeing the LORD has departed from you and has become your enemy? And the LORD has done for Himself as He spoke to me. For the LORD has torn the kingdom out of your hand and given it to your neighbor, David. Because you did not obey the voice of the LORD nor execute His fierce wrath upon Amole, therefore, the LORD has done this thing to you this day. Moreover, the LORD will also deliver you with Israel into the hand of the Philistines. And tomorrow you and your sons will be with me.*"

1 Chronicles 10, closes with theses words: "*So Saul died for his unfaithfulness which he committed against the Lord, because he did not keep the Word of the Lord, and also because he consulted a medium for guidance. But he did not inquire of the LORD; therefore He killed him, and turned the kingdom over to David the son of Jesse.*"

Saul's death may fall into the category of *the sin unto death*. The essence of the meaning of the *sin unto death* is when a child of God lives so degradingly and disgustingly before God that in an act of mercy God takes the person home. That is the sin unto death. Do not confuse it with the *unpardonable sin*. A Christian *cannot commit the unpardonable sin*, but *only a Christian can commit the sin unto death*.

The age-old question is: *was Saul saved?* There is the theological viewpoint that allows the conclusion that Saul lost his salvation. However, it is not an accurate conclusion. In the prophet's announcement Samuel clearly said, "*Tomorrow you and your sons are going to be with me.*"

In Old Testament times the place for the departed spirits of the saints was called *Shell*. Samuel informed Saul he and his sons would be *with him*. However, this visit of Samuel's spirit from the spirit-world is not confirmation, neither is it permission, to attempt to reach those who have departed. This appearance of

Samuel was permitted within the realm of God's sovereignty and omniscience.

The Pathetic Acceptance

After hearing the pronouncement of his death, Saul fell to the ground in dreadful fear. The story is told about a Christian general in World War I who wrote about how some unsaved men faced their deaths in battle, compared to how some Christians faced their deaths. He said he could hear unsaved men in their foxholes cursing the Germans, loading their rifles, throwing grenades, and fighting with all their strength, while some Christians were hunkered down, whimpering, and crying in the face of death. *That is a description of Pathetic Acceptance.*

Saul's acceptance of the announcement of his death was pathetic. A better response than *pathetic acceptance* is personal acceptance. The Bible presents case after case where people turned to God in the face of their impending death. Saul represents people who squander their opportunity for God to extend His grace.

Jonah prayed and was extended grace. Joshaphat prayed and was extended grace. The classic return of the Prodigal Son is the graphic example of accepting extended grace.

God would rather *save us* than *sentence us.* God would rather *comfort us* than *condemn us.* It is amazing to me how some people choose to *die* rather than to be *delivered.* Like too many people, Saul lived beneath his privilege and ultimately died beneath his privilege.

SAUL'S DEATH

Chapter Fifteen

1 Samuel 31: 1-7; 2 Samuel 1: 1-27

On several occasions David's Godly qualities rose to the surface. His reaction to the news of Saul's death was another time when those qualities came to the surface. In its own way a death notice is a test of our spiritual quality. It's like a dipstick that is plunged into the engine of a car to measure the oil level. Who the death notice is for determines the degree of the test. It's not only a matter of who died but also how the person died that tests us. And, the closer we are to the person who has died will to a large degree determine how we will react to the death notice.

Nevertheless, *closeness* to the deceased person is not the only test of our spiritual qualities; the *coldness* we may have felt toward the decedent when he or she was alive might also test our spiritual qualities in a number of ways. It is not only the good relationship that we had with a person that tests our spiritual qualities, it can also be the bad relationship that we had with a person that tests them. The death notice of an enemy simply tests our spiritual qualities at a different level.

If we are devastated at the death of a *family member* or *friend*, and *delighted* at the death of a *foe*, we didn't pass the test. There are some people who, if they had been in David's shoes, would have thrown a celebration when they heard that Saul was dead. Talk about celebration time; some people would have had a party and with glass raised high toasted saying, "I'm glad you're dead and gone, you rascal you, and sorry you stayed so long." But, that wasn't the case with David. When David heard the news of Saul's death, his Godly qualities rose to the surface. He grieved as if he had lost a family member or a dear friend.

In honest retrospect, we must conclude that Saul's tragic death was not totally his fault. From the beginning he did not want to be king. As best he could, he tried to avoid becoming king. However, because of the insistence of the people he reluctantly consented against his will. He even went into hiding, but they came and took him out of hiding and made him king.

Here is a quote worth remembering: "*When a person tells you he or she is not good enough for you, believe it*." Hey brother, when a sister tells you she's not good enough for you, believe her! Sister girl, when that hunk of a guy tells you he doesn't think he's good enough for you, you had better believe him! He knows more about himself than you do!

The point is, in many ways, Saul tried to tell Israel not to make him king, but they chose him anyway – and they chose him primarily because of his physical appearance. This is not unlike people in church who thrust leadership positions upon their friends because they like them. The blatant truth is that just because someone is a friend does not mean he or she has the qualities for being a spiritual leader in the church. Notwithstanding, Saul was ultimately responsible for his behavior as king, but the people were responsible for putting him in the position.

As time revealed, Saul had an unyielding disobedient spirit. When Saul made up his mind that he wasn't going to do something, it was futile to try to make him change his mind. When Saul made up his mind that he was going to do something, it was also futile to try to make him change his mind.

Not even the prophet of God, with word from God, could change Saul's mind. When Saul determined that he was right, it didn't matter how obviously wrong he was, he was not going to change. When Saul took a position on an issue, even after he realized he was on the wrong side and had made the wrong decision, he was not about to change. This was highlighted (or low-lighted) by four glaring, obstinate, obscene acts of disobedience.

The first occasion was when he took the priest's place and offered the sacrifice. He disregarded the place of the man of God by thinking that Samuel was late and would not arrive in time to offer the sacrifice. So he did the sacrifice himself.

Also, he wasn't supposed to take any prisoners after his victory over the Amalekites, but he saved the king alive. Neither was he supposed to take any of the spoils from the battle, but he kept the best of the cattle and the other beasts.

And, there was the time when he ordered the slaughter of all the priests in Israel – eighty-five priests, their wives, children, and their children's children. The entire city of Nob was annihilated, leaving only one priest, who escaped to David for safety.

Last, he sought consultation with a witch for direction for his life. Saul did all of that with never a time of recanting or repenting.

As you can see, these four incidents do not include his mistreatment of David. He did all the above and not one time was there a word of repentance from Saul. According to 1 Chronicles 10: 13-14, the consultation with the witch was the transgression that cost him his life: "*So Saul died for his unfaithfulness which he had committed against the Lord, because he did not keep the word of the*

Lord, **and also because he consulted a medium for guidance**."

His death was the fulfillment of the prophecy of Samuel.

Saul died on the mountainside of Gilboa. The biblical record indicates several archers mortally wounded him in battle. Several arrows pierced him through and, for fear that the Philistines would kill him and abuse his body, he ordered his armor bearer to thrust him through with his spear so he would not die at the hands of the enemy.

He was selfish and self-centered even to the end.

Ironically, after he died the Philistines still abused his body. That is what they always did with the dead bodies of their enemies. When Saul's armor bearer refused to kill him, he leaned upon his spear and took his own life. Out of perverted devotion to his king, the armor bearer also took his own life.

The Tale of the Runner

There were, of course, no cell phones, Email or fax machines in those days. Runners were used to bring and carry urgent news. The men who had that profession were said to have "beautiful feet." That is the imagery Paul used in Romans 10:15: "*How beautiful are the feet of them who preach the Gospel and bring glad tidings of good news.*"

But, the runner who brought the news of Saul's death to David was not a professional runner. He was, as the story reveals, a scheming opportunist.

Astute bible readers will notice what appears to be an inconsistency about how Saul died in 1 Samuel 31 and 2 Samuel 1. Chapter 31 of 1 Samuel indicates that Saul killed himself, but Chapter 1 of 2 Samuel indicates that this runner killed Saul. However, what seems to be an inconsistency dissipates with some rather obvious observations. The first light of suspicion is when the runner came and did obeisance unto David. That is an act of greeting that is appropriate only for royalty. It is to bow one's self down to the ground. The interesting thing is that none of the other guys in David's camp had been bowing down to him.

Then he proceeded to tell David that Saul was dead and that

he had performed the deed at Saul's request. He made it appear to be a mercy killing (euthanasia is nothing new). He told David, "I stood over him and killed him because I was sure that he could not live after he had fallen. And I took the crown that was on his head and the bracelet that was on his arm, and have brought them unto my lord."

Notwithstanding, it is highly unlikely that Saul would summon him to take his life because Amalekites had no better standing in Israel than Philistines; in fact they may have had lesser standing than Philistines. A plausible explanation is that some of what he says was true, such as where he says, "*I happened by chance to be passing by.*" He was probably passing by the battlefield and heard the conversation between Saul and his armor bearer. Then he saw Saul take his life, and later saw his armor bearer take his own life. But he embellished the story by saying he killed Saul. In other words, he lied and put himself in the center of the story to ingratiate himself to David.

The Touching Remorse

David's remorse is the spiritual quality that rose to the surface to which I alluded earlier. The spiritual quality is the fact that David actually felt remorse for Saul at his death; the fact that he mourned for Saul. A person with lesser spiritual qualities would not have been able to fake or feign sadness for Saul. David genuinely grieved for Saul. His mourning was displayed in the customary manner of the culture of his day. The custom of the eastern culture was to rip and tear one's clothing and sometimes to sprinkle dirt upon one's head. "*Therefore, David took hold of his own clothes and tore them, and so did all the men who were with him. And they mourned and wept and fasted until evening for Saul and Jonathan, his son.*"

Note that the word "fasted" (*tsoom*) is not used in the sense where one would particularly or intentionally refrain from food. Instead, the meaning is to have no appetite for food. A true sign of a grieving person is when there is no appetite.

Also, note the dimensions of his remorse were for Saul,

Jonathan, the people of God, and for the house of Israel. Don't miss that. Note particularly that David mourned for the people of God *and* for the house of Israel. David had a deep perception of God and also a deep perception of the people of God, and discerned that all the people of God were not of the house of Israel.

David knew that God had other people (Gentiles) who called on His name who were not among the people of Israel. After all, David had relatives in Moab. That's significant because it indicates how far ahead David was of his theological time. In the days of Jesus no respectable Jew would go through Samaria into Gentile territory, but David knew that God had other people beside the house of Israel, so he mourned for the people of God in general, and for the house of Israel in particular.

I would love to have seen the look on that Amalekite's face when he saw David tear his clothes and start weeping and wailing. His reaction was probably like when someone attempts to tell you some juicy *new gossip* and you indicate you're not interested – and the person you're telling looks at you like you're crazy. A second attempt is made, this time emphasizing that it is new gossip, not the same old gossip that other gossipers are telling, and the person just can't believe you don't want to hear it.

This guy thought he was going to ingratiate himself to David by bringing him the crown. He wanted the designation and the distinction of being known in Israel as the man who brought David the crown – the man who helped David to get to the throne. But, if he had seen David in the cave when he refused to take Saul's life, he wouldn't have been surprised to see David's remorse when he heard the news of Saul's death.

People of ordinary heart are delighted when their enemy has fallen or been crushed, but David was not a man of ordinary heart. *He was a man after God's own heart.*

David reminds me of Joseph when his brethren, who had sold him into slavery, had to face him to buy grain. The Bible says Joseph could not control himself and wept aloud. I probably would have been looking for some rocks to throw at them!

Take a personal test right here. Have you ever had an occasion when you thought you would enjoy hearing some bad news about someone, but when you heard it you, instead, felt sadness? It was news you thought would bring you joy, but upon hearing it you felt shame and sorrow for the person.

Back in the days of Richard Millhouse Nixon and the Watergate scandal, it was announced when he was going to give his resignation. I remember it like it was yesterday. I did not go to the office that day. I canceled my appointments because I wanted to personally see the no good rascal resign. I pulled my chair right up in front of the television set, because I was going to get my money's worth that day.

However, when President Nixon concluded his resignation speech, tears were in my eyes and a lump was in my throat. I was embarrassed and felt empathy for him because he was *my* president. Even though I had not voted for him, he was still my president.

Perhaps you have had a similar experience. If you've had an experience like that, then cultivate that Godly quality. And if you haven't, plant the seed in your heart so you can start to cultivate it.

There is New Testament Scripture for what David did. David's performance was far beyond the Old Testament standard. Jesus said, "*Bless those who curse you and do good to those who despitefully use you.*" Paul appropriately warns us, "*Let him who thinks he stands take heed lest he fall.*" If we are part of a plot or a ploy to bring someone down, or rejoice in the downfall of another person, shame on us.

The Tough Retribution

When David had regained his composure, he asked the runner who he was and where he had come from. The man replied, **"I am the son of a sojourner. I am an Amalekite."** Then David asked him, "*Why were you not afraid to touch the Lord's anointed?*"

The Apostle Paul developed a strong theology around that question – insisting that Christians always treat the man of God with reverence and respect. The question for our time could be,

"You mean to tell me that you are not afraid to talk all kinds of loose talk behind the back of the man of God, whom God has placed over you?"

The question for Christians would be, "You mean you're not afraid to get on the telephone and engage in all kinds of random gossip and rumors about the Man of God? You mean you are not scared?"

For us it would be, "You mean you're not afraid to refuse to follow the leadership and the vision of the pastor whom the Holy Spirit has made overseer of this flock?"

It is definitely a question for our time. Much of the irreverent talk and resentment of a pastor amounts to "touching the man of God."

It doesn't appear that David was convinced this man had killed Saul. I take that stance based on the fact that David was wise. Wisdom was one of the characteristics David displayed early on, so he wasn't fooled by this fabricated story. But, even though the man didn't kill Saul, his admission that he did is what condemned him. David ordered his execution immediately by one of his soldiers. The last words he heard were those of David saying, "*You should never touch the Lord's anointed.*"

This was tough retribution. Twenty-first century people may even call it excessive retribution. Incidences like this appear to be grossly inhumane and Bible critics use them to discredit the Word of God. The retribution ordered by David must be understood in the context of the theological times of the Old Testament. Then it was "*an eye for an eye, hand for hand, foot for foot, bruising for bruising and burning for burning.*" David's behavior on many occasions exceeded the standard for New Testament saints.

The Tender Resolution

David wrote a tender resolution in honor and memory of King Saul. It was similar to a funeral resolution. It was a touching eulogy. It began with a declaration: "*The glory of Israel is slain among the high places: how are the mighty fallen.*" A better translation is: "*The honor of Israel has been slain.*"

It included deprecation: "*Tell it not in Gath and publish it not in the streets of Ashkelon lest the daughters of the Philistines rejoice, lest the daughters of uncircumcised triumph.*"

Gath and Ashkelon were major Philistine cities. He didn't want his people to announce the news to their enemies. Sometimes the people of God are guilty of sharing sensitive information with unbelievers that should remain only among the household of faith. Many Christians eagerly, and unwisely, participate in conversations with unbelievers about matters damaging to the witness of the church.

There was also desolation in the resolution it was as if David pointed his finger toward Mount Gilboa (the place of Saul's death) when he said, "*You mountains of Gilboa, let there be no dew, neither let there be rain upon you, nor fields of offerings; for the shield of the mighty is vilely cast away, the shield of Saul, as though he had not been anointed with oil.*"

On my first trip to Israel, as we were headed south from Jerusalem to Jericho, the tour guide called our attention to the barren top of Mount Gilboa and referenced David's eulogy of Saul. At this point David's words became prophetical as well as eulogistically. Lest we forget, David was also prophet. He prophesied the birth, death, and resurrection of the Messiah in his many Psalms. Since David spoke those words, no trees have grown on Mount Gilboa. It is barren. The Government of Israel has recently started a program of reforestation of the mountains of Gilboa.

The eulogy is also marked by dedication unto Saul and Jonathan. He continued with these words: "*From the blood of the slain from the fat of the mighty, the bow of Jonathan turned not back, and the sword of Saul returned not empty. Saul and Jonathan were lovely and pleasant in their lives, and in their death they were not divided; they were swifter than eagles, they were stronger than lions.*"

Imagine that.

David spoke of both Saul and Jonathan as being "lovely." There is that Godly quality of David again. It caused him to say only good about Saul in his death and nothing bad.

There is also designation. He gave instruction to the women: "*You daughters of Israel, weep over Saul, who clothed you with scarlet, with other delights, who put ornaments of gold upon your apparel.*"

He admonished the women of Israel to start crying, whether they wanted to cry or not, because their king was dead.

Last of all, there is delineation. He spoke about his friendship and fellowship with Jonathan with these tender words: "*How are the mighty fallen in the midst of battle! O Jonathan, your high places.*"

Put yourself in David's place. If you were called upon to write a resolution, or to give a eulogy for someone who had made you the object of threats and attacks for most of your life, how would you handle it? If you had to say some nice words about someone who had maligned your character and misrepresented your God-given purpose, what would you do?

Could you do it? Before you answer, let me help you, particularly if your answer is "no." A better answer than saying "no" would be to say, "not in my own strength." Understand, please, David did not say this eulogy in his own strength. In Psalms 27:1 he says, "*The Lord is the strength of my life.*" And in Psalms 46:1 he says, "*God is our refuge and our strength.*"

The reason David spoke in such glowing words about Saul at his death was because *he had forgiven Saul.* That's also the reason David mourned so remorsefully for Saul. *He had forgiven him.* And it's also the reason David cried genuine sorrowful tears. *He had forgiven him.*

When bad news about your enemy gives you *satisfaction* instead of *sorrow*, it means you have not forgiven him or her. And, it means you need to be released from what was done to you. Release comes when you forgive the person who hurt you.

Some people carry the *baggage* and *bondage* of old hurts and wounds from childhood to adulthood. Sometimes the person who injured them is dead, yet their emotions are still fractured. I have sent some people to the grave of a deceased person so they could verbally express their forgiveness.

Even after a person is dead a verbal expression of forgiveness will psychologically relieve the burden of anger, guilt, and shame. You must release it to be whole, because when you *live in your past* you *limit blessings* that are coming in your future. Forgiveness is not a sign of weakness; it's a sign of strength. Forgiveness does more for the *forgiver* than the *forgiven*.

Furthermore, there may be an occasion where we will have to forgive when the offender won't ask to be forgiven. Some people can't or won't ask for forgiveness. If Saul did not ask God to forgive him, it's unlikely that he asked David to forgive him? Yet, when David heard the news that Saul was dead, he mourned genuinely and publicly for him. It's another indication of David's Godly qualities.

ON TO THE THRONE

Chapter Sixteen

2 Samuel 2:1-11

The second chapter of 2 Samuel is not only a new chapter in the historical twin book; it is also a new chapter in David's life. The record of Scripture shows God had destined David to be the next king of Israel when he was a boy, and finally the time had come. The time of waiting was over. Saul's death, in particular, signaled that the time had eventually come. David could now go on the throne.

What God destines for us often takes time to come to fruition. It is crucial that we learn to accept God's timing instead of our own. The timing for David to finally go on to the throne was many years after he was anointed to be king. It had been a long time since that fateful day when Samuel showed up at Jesse's house with the unannounced intention of anointing the next King of Israel. The passing of all those years since that day must have seemed like a vague dream to David. However, at long last the moment of his kingship had arrived.

Time is a great teacher, and most Christians have learned that God's timing is perfect. After a while we come to know and appreciate God's timing. I can personally confess how grateful I am for every delay the Lord orchestrated in my life. I praise God for every postponement He arranged in my destiny. I now realize I was not necessarily waiting on God, but He was actually waiting for me. God was waiting for me to develop my maturity, and to deepen my capacity for understanding, so that I could handle His blessings. And, I'm certain this isn't my personal observation exclusively; it is, probably, also your observation.

You are now, no doubt, enjoying blessings of God that if placed in your possession at an earlier time would have resulted in disaster. So God waits for us, and with the passing of time we slowly develop the capacity of gratitude and appreciation for why God has waited.

Lest we forget, David was a teenager when Samuel came to his father's house and anointed him to be king. However, at the time of the text he was approximately thirty years old, which proves that it is worth it to wait for God's best. Our waiting will not be in vain when we receive His best. All those years were a fair exchange when David went on the throne.

The Cautious Request

Before making a move toward the throne, however, David inquired cautiously of God if it was time. Perhaps his many unwise past choices motivated him to first ask God first before going ahead on his own. You may recall that David had taken some faulty and foolish steps while he was fleeing from Saul.

Those decisions made without prayer may have been part of his inspiration for writing Psalms 37:23: "*The steps of a good man are ordered by the Lord.*"

He now had the equity of maturity that restrained him from

taking any action until after he sought counsel of God. The natural propensity of people is to turn to God in the time of *immense trouble*, but not necessarily to turn to Him in the time of *imminent triumph*. For some reason it is easier for us to pray to God when experiencing *adversity* than to pray to Him when we are experiencing *prosperity*.

It is seemingly easier to pray to God when there is a possibility of a *demotion* than to pray to Him when there is a possibility of *promotion*. It is easier to pray to God when you are about to lose a *position* than to pray to Him when you are about to be *lifted to a position*. It is easier to pray when things are *not* going right than when things *are* going right. So we witness David's *caution* at a time when many people would be *careless*.

We are typically impatient about a position we think we deserve, not realizing, obviously, that any position or blessing is given to us by the grace of God. David didn't respond that way. He took time to pray about the position God had already guaranteed to him, which is commendable. It was, after all, a position he had been anointed for about sixteen years earlier.

He did not pray about *taking* the position, rather about the *timing* for taking the position. And he prayed about the *tenure* of the position. The specific words of his prayer were: "*Shall I go up to one of the cities in Judah*?"

He sought direction from God because he needed the location as to where he was to initiate his reign as King. He apparently had the sense that his kingdom would be established someplace in Judah. God undoubtedly had revealed that much to him. The quandary was about where in Judah would his capital city be located.

Here is something to always remember: the more *choices* we have, the more *chances* we have of making a mistake. So David prayed. He needed instruction and direction from God about *when* and *where* he was to initiate his kingdom.

The Clear Response

The *cautious request* resulted in a *clear response* from God. A

New Testament warning says *we have not because we ask not.* It is not practical to expect a clear response from God if there has not been a clear request. The first problem is not asking: *we have not because we ask not.*

The second problem is not asking specifically: "*But when you pray, you pray amiss.*" "Praying amiss" is praying pointlessly, meaninglessly, and without specificity. My goodness, if we are going to bother to use energy for praying, we may as well use it to pray for something specific. Many of the requests we make to God are for collective blessings that God is going to confer upon us anyway.

David prayed clearly and the Lord answered him clearly. David's clear request was: "*Shall I go up*?" And God's response was: "*Go up.*"

That's clear and concise by anyone's estimation. David apparently realized that he hadn't prayed as specifically as he could have so he then asked, "*Where shall I go up*?" Since David became more precise in his request, God became more precise in His response. God replied with two more words: "*unto Hebron.*"

Granted, sometimes communication from God is rather vague, but this is really plain. It's hard to misunderstand what God is saying when He has only spoken two words: "*Go up*" followed by two more words, "*unto Hebron.*"

Who couldn't get that straight? Who would have a problem understanding those instructions and following those directions? You don't have to be a Christian for forty years to understand that.

"*Shall I go up*?"

"*Go up.*"

"*Where shall I go up*?"

"*Unto Hebron.*"

No one needs a six-month seminary course to understand that. God spoke plainly to David.

A simple but wise conclusion is that when God says go to a place we would be wise to go to that place. When God gives us instructions about a person, we would be wise to heed that instruction. When God gives directions about a *pursuit*, we would be smart to listen to what He says about that pursuit.

We should listen to God, whether it's about *a place, a person* or *a pursuit.*

Lest we forget, Hebron was the burial place for Abraham and Sarah. That gave David's place for his kingdom *historical* and *memorial* significance.

The next words recorded after God responded to David are: "*So David went there.*" Unlike some of us (myself included), David followed God's instructions. He went there.

A true confession is warranted here. I don't always go where God wants me to go or do what He wants me to do. Nevertheless, a clear response from God should get a confident reaction from us. *So David went there.*

There is a particularly valuable illustration here for parents. David was also leading a family. He had two wives and some small children when he went to Hebron. Parents should follow David's example of thoroughly praying before moving their family. Not only was David leading a family, he was leading a following. He had more than six hundred men with their families following his leadership.

The Cunning Rebellion

Abner, the captain of Saul's army, orchestrated a cunning rebellion. He had arranged for Ishbosheth (one of the lesser known sons of Saul) to become king. Remember, Jonathan was in line to become king in natural succession after Saul. Since Jonathan was dead, it meant the succession naturally, and rightfully, went to the oldest living son.

Where did Ishbosheth come from and who was he? He did not have direct access to the throne. Abner's maneuver to make Ishbosheth king occurred either before David went to Hebron, while he was en route to Hebron, or after he had arrived in Hebron. It was a counter-movement to the revelation God had given David.

Abner's position was "Captain of the Host" under Saul. David's Captain was a man named Joab. The position was a mix between what we now have as the Secretary of Defense and the Chairman of the Joint Chiefs of Staff. It was a very powerful and prestigious position.

Now consider this: many people in the kingdom knew that David was God's choice to be the next king, so how was it that Abner didn't know? In fact, even the enemies of Israel knew they would someday have to deal with David. So why didn't Abner know?

The truth is, he *did*, which is why it was a cunning rebellion. Nevertheless, Abner's rebellion was amateurish compared to what Joab would do later on. (These two Captains will interface in a rather interesting way later on).

David had no one more loyal to him than Joab. Joab possessed pristine loyalty to David, but the problem was that he was so crooked in dealing with others on David's behalf that he embarrassed David many times. Joab was void of the basic characteristics of integrity.

It's a leader's nightmare to have someone who is faithful and loyal, but who has a personal agenda that is working against the leader's agenda. Loyalty from a subordinate is what a leader needs, but a leader should be able to trust the subordinate. This was David's problem with Joab: he couldn't trust his judgment.

Abner pulled off his political maneuver, but David's prayers negated it. We can't control the cunning maneuvers of people around us, but we can pray. We can't control the deceitful actions of people we work or serve with, but we can pray. You can't stop people from undermining your good name and your God-given purpose, but you can pray. In light of the cunning rebellion described in these Scriptures, we can see the powerful results of effectual fervent prayer.

The Crown with Restrictions

David eventually was crowned King, but his coronation was with restrictions. His kingdom was restricted to the perimeters of Judah. This means that after running, hiding, and sleeping in caves for nearly sixteen years, when it came time to be anointed king, he was made King of Judah only. The territory of Judah was the smaller portion of Israel.

Fortunately, David's spiritual capacity enabled him to handle *disappointments* as well *appointments*. For the time being, even though he was King of Judah only, he still had the promise of God that he would be King of Israel. After nearly sixteen years of waiting, he still had to wait a little longer.

David had his share of disappointments, as we all do. Disappointment makes up a realistic portion of our existence. A line from one of the many award-winning poems by Langston Hughes is when the mother says to her son: "Life for me ain't been no crystal stair." It means that she had faced many disappointments in her life. Real life, not Hollywood life, BET life, or HBO life is permeated with disappointments and, not only permeated, but also sometimes saturated.

Disappointments are as much a part of living as is success. The duration of David's kingship over Judah is revealed in these words: "*And the time that David was king in Hebron over the house of Judah was seven and one-half years.*" Seven and one-half years is approximately half the time that he waited to become King of Judah. After waiting nearly sixteen years, he had another wait of seven and one-half years.

Not only does God tell us to wait sometimes, be sometimes tells us to wait even longer. You may long to know when your tests and trials will finally come to an end, but the fact is that you may have to wait some more for the answer. You may have to continue saying, "When it rains it pours."

You may ask, "When is my breakthrough coming?" And the Lord may answer, "You have to wait some more."

You may ask, "When will the door of opportunity open for me like it has for so many of my friends? And your answer may be, "You have to wait."

So your resolve should be to wait for the Lord's timing, not your own. You wanted your blessing yesterday, but it may not be today or anytime soon. Nevertheless, your resolve, and my resolve, should be to wait for the Lord's timing.

It is in one of David's psalms where he says: "*Wait on the Lord and be of good courage.*"

And, don't cuss at the dog or kick the cat while you're waiting. If you could speak to the Psalmist and ask him how a person can be of good courage while waiting on the Lord, he would answer: "*He shall strengthen your heart.*"

Isaiah's version of waiting for God goes like this: "*They that wait upon the Lord shall renew their strength.*" It's very similar to what David said. We are supposed to see that there is a connection between gaining strength and waiting on the Lord. We would not get stronger if we didn't sometimes wait on the Lord. You would, in fact, be as weak as you were last year if every now and then He did not make you wait. "*They that wait upon the Lord shall renew their strength. They shall mount up with wings as an eagle. They shall run and not be weary. They shall walk and not faint.*"

It seems unfair almost that after all David had gone through; when he was finally anointed king it was with restrictions. He reined only over the land of Judah. However, he had the assurance and promise of God that he would be King of all Israel. The promises of God are our best assurances. David patiently waited for God to provide the opportunity for him to become King of Israel, and his waiting was not in vain.

DAVID BECOMES KING OVER ALL ISRAEL

Chapter Seventeen

2 Samuel 5:1-10

Without exception this portion of David's life is also rich in instruction and inspiration for our personal application. This segment of David's life (when he became king) is as significant for our edification as when he was a shepherd boy, and when he was fleeing and hiding from Saul. It is relevant for Christians today.

In the previous chapter we saw that David was first anointed King of Judah only. However, seven and one-half years later he became king over the other ten tribes, which finally made him King of Israel. A point for our edification is that David's move to the throne came after many delays and after many years between the delays.

How excited would you be about having to wait seven and one-half years for some special blessing?

One of the ladies in our church called to inform me that she was retuning to college and to ask for my prayers. She said, "Pastor, I am going to be seventy-two years old when I finish college." And I said, "Yes, but you're going to be seventy-two in four years whether you finish college or not."

Her choice was to be seventy-two years old *with* a college degree or to be seventy-two years old *without* a college degree. Four more years would be added to her age whether she retuned to college or not.

How many people do you know who can wait patiently and expectantly for seven and one-half years to buy a house? Some people have to wait that long to get out of prison. Seven and one-half years is a long time when you are looking *forward* to it. It doesn't seem as long when you are looking backward to it.

David waited seven and one-half *more* years before he became King of Israel and, what's more, the hand of God orchestrated all of those delays en route to the throne.

Numerous concerns, complaints, and circumstances are represented in each of our lives. We would like to have had them resolved last week, but chances are there are still lingering, nagging unsolved problems in all our lives. However, as people of God, we should always remember His timing is perfect. When all is said and done, we have to admit that we can't improve upon God's timing at all.

After we acknowledge that God can, and will, orchestrate delays in our lives, we must also admit that we can cause delays on our own. We can, on our own, arrange the postponement of blessings. Most of the time, in fact, it's not God's delays we experience; it's our own. We have become expert at self-imposed delays and postponement of blessings.

It's important that we recognize and understand that a lot of events transpired during the seven and one-half years when David was King of Judah only. Abner was killed and a civil war broke out between the two kingdoms (needless to say, David's side won). Ishbosheth was also killed.

Granted, it was not right the way Abner died, but it was also not right how he went about on his own to make a king over Israel in David's place. It was not right how Ishbosheth died, but it was also not right how he let Abner make him king when he knew David was to be the king. It's sort of like the adage, "What goes around comes around."

David, out of the deep capacity of his heart, mourned the deaths of both Abner and Ishbosheth. A man of lesser heart would not have mourned them. The day they died was not a day of rejoicing for David. It may have been a day of rejoicing for others, but not for David. News of their deaths was not good news to him. Therefore, the men who thought they would receive a reward from David when they brought him Ishbosheth's head were surprised by his reaction. He informed them that he had already had one man killed for claiming to have killed King Saul. And he gave them the same reception. *David never did anything of a self-promoting nature to become king, not when he became King of Judah or King of Israel.*

The Crown of Confirmation

"*Then all the tribes of Israel came to David at Hebron.*" This means all the tribes represented by their elders. The representatives numbered in the hundreds. This was an impressive, massive gathering of people and speaks of calculated, conscientious commitment on their parts. Furthermore, it implies they had already met together in agreement before coming to David. All that was next required was to meet with David and to offer him the overall kingdom.

It's said that hindsight is twenty-twenty. Since that is true, this move to make David the overall king fit God's plan for him to first be king over Judah only. The benefit was that it gave the other ten tribes time to observe David as a king. They had opportunity to see that God's hand was upon his life and upon his leadership.

They saw David's kingdom being blessed while their kingdom was becoming less. And, of course, the civil war they had lost to David didn't hurt his chances for becoming king over all the tribes. Actually, losing the war helped them make up their minds that David should be their king. So they offered David the crown to be over the United Kingdom.

It was both a *confirmation* and also their *confession* to David; that he had been the right man for the job all along. It's noble when people can admit their misjudgment of someone. A lot of people can't do that. They can't admit that they are wrong, or that they misjudged someone's ability or character.

In the early years of my pastorate, several people who doubted my leadership left in obvious protest. Some joined other churches and some are not in any church today. None of them have come back to say that they made a mistake.

Consequently, this was a noble gesture by these tribal representatives. I admire people who can come back and say, "I misjudged you. I made a mistake." These leaders gave three reasons for their decision. Only one was needed, but they gave three.

First they said, "*We are your bone and your flesh.*" This means they were relatives. It's important that we understand that people in Bible days were basically no different than people in our day. Like people in our time they began with small talk. People who need to apologize often begin with small talk. A prelude of small talk is typical of people who dread having to say they were wrong. If kinship is a factor the person most likely will begin by saying, "*Now you know we are kin.*" An admission of kinship is a buffer for the dreaded apology. In this case, who else could be king over Israel except another Israelite? Their first reason was so obvious they didn't need to articulate it.

Their second reason was the record. Continuing, they said, "*When Saul was king over us, you were the one who led Israel out and brought them in; and the LORD said to you, 'You shall shepherd My people Israel, and be ruler over Israel.'"*

That reminds me of an interview a cocky reporter had with Rev. Ralph Abernathy after the death of Dr. Martin Luther King, Jr. Rev. Abernathy had become the President of the Southern Leadership Conference in the absence of Dr. King. Obviously, after the death of Dr. King the Civil Rights Movement waned a bit and lost some of its momentum. And this cocky reporter was trying to imply that the movement had slowed down because something was lacking with Rev. Abernathy's leadership.

Rev. Abernathy responded succinctly by saying, "Martin had an Abernathy. I could do more if I had an Abernathy." Rev. Abernathy had been the inestimable right hand behind the scenes for Dr. King. Dr. King had the personality for the movement, but Rev. Abernathy had the push for the movement. History shows they were an awesome pair. While Dr. King was "doing his thing" *publicly*, Rev. Abernathy was "doing his thing" *secretly*.

So these tribal representatives were admitting to David that he was the man behind the scenes who was really getting the job done in the shadow of King Saul.

Their third reason was the *revelation*. It actually should have been the first and only reason they needed. It was the revelation of God that David would be the next king over Israel. They admitted that David was supposed to be their king because of the revelation of God.

What else do you need once God has spoken? What else is there after God has spoken? I know what we often do after God has spoken. *We do what we want to do.* Nevertheless, all they needed to say to David was, "We are here to accept you as king because you are God's choice to be king." They expressed it precisely: "*The LORD said to you, 'You shall shepherd My people Israel, and be ruler over Israel.'*" The Lord also said, "*You shall feed my people Israel and you shall be captain over my people.*"

The meaning of "feed" has nothing to do with physical food.

And, the word for "captain" in Hebrew means literally "shepherd." It refers to the spiritual dimension of the King of Israel. The King of Israel had a spiritual dimension of responsibility and a civil dimension. Saul was severely lacking in that spiritual dimension. He did not shepherd God's people, so they made a league, or a covenant, with David.

The offer of the crown was also confirmation that David was God's choice by revelation to be King of Israel.

The Challenge of Contempt

David set his sights on Jerusalem to be capital of his kingdom. However, there was a problem with David's desire and decision to make Jerusalem his capital city. The problem was the Jebusites, who had used Jerusalem as their stronghold dating all the way back to the days of Joshua, and the Jebusites were the most resistant of all the Canaanite people to Israel's occupation of the land. Consequently, they were the most stubborn when it came to being removed out of Canaan, and their strength and resistance was primarily because of the stronghold they had at Jerusalem.

A geographical description of Jerusalem is given in Psalm 122: "*Jerusalem is built as a city that is compact together, where the tribes go up.*" Joshua 15:63 also says, "*As for the Jebusites, the inhabitants of Jerusalem, the children of Judah could not drive them out; but the Jebusites dwell with the children of Judah at Jerusalem to this day.*"

Apparently, in as much as the Jebusites were entrenched in Jerusalem, Israel had resolved to coexist with them. The Jebusites gave the challenge of contempt in the form of a dare to David and his men. Paraphrasing their challenge, they essentially said, "You couldn't get past the blind and the lame to come in here."

Our younger generation calls that "talking smack." It meant that David could not take Jerusalem if their sentries were blind and lame. That was glaring contempt. They, perhaps, had good reason to feel so confidently secure, because Joshua in his heyday couldn't take Jerusalem – and Joshua was one of God's bad boys. In all the history of Israel, no captain or commander fielded an army that could take Jerusalem, so their contemptuous challenge was based on that historical fact.

The Conquest of Courage

Immediately following their challenge the Bible reads, "*Nevertheless, David took the stronghold.*"

Those five words speak volumes of inspiration about "possibilities" beating "impossibilities," and about winning against overwhelming odds. It means that regardless of history being on the side of their opposition, David still took the city. It means, regardless of the failed record of attempts by other attackers, David still took the city.

That really blesses my soul. Anyone who has had victories in life is victorious because he or she didn't listen to all the speculations about failure, or accusations that they couldn't make it. You are where you are because you wouldn't give in to speculation and accusations of failure. But, more importantly, you are who you are because you wouldn't fold under the pressure of negative talk.

You're a third- or fourth-year college student with no resources because you wouldn't give in. You're a single parent with two, three, or four children, yet you maintain a household on one income because you wouldn't give in. You've learned how to stretch meals. You could teach Martha Stewart some things in *her* kitchen. You've become a homemaker economist.

You're who you are, between jobs. Some days you have a job, some days you don't, but you haven't given up. You're who you are. You've got a job with sub-standard pay and a bunch of missing paychecks, but God has met your every need.

You're who you are; a senior citizen college student with grandchildren who is just starting, but you're not going to quit until you flip your tassel and hold that degree in your hand. You've seen a lot of people cave in around you, but you wouldn't recant or hold back. Some of David's spirit is in you because you've forged ahead when others were advising you to stop.

David, you see, was not deterred by the fact that no other commander, including Joshua, had taken the city. He first of all figured out a strategy for taking Jerusalem.

It was how Mohammed Ali mastered each opponent he faced before the fight ever began. Ali had a gift, a knack of finding a weak spot in the offense or the defense of his opponent, which he capitalized on to win.

David saw something that no other commander or captain had ever seen. When David looked at Jerusalem with all its fortified strengths, he also saw a weakness.

"What was it?" you ask.

It was the location and position of the water shaft. Joshua had seen that same water shaft, but he didn't see what David saw when he looked at it. David saw an offensive advantage in the location of the shaft. So he gave his men a positive challenge to counter-balance the negative challenge they had received from the Jebusites.

David's challenge was that whoever got to the water shaft first would have the perfect position to lead them to victory. And, he attached an incentive to his challenge: whoever reached the water shaft first would be his chief and captain.

It's important to recognize principles of leadership when they show up in a biblical narrative. Leadership is, and always has been, a critical commodity for the people of God. But, it's equally as critical to point out principles of followership.

There is a principle of followership that almost leaps off the pages of this narrative. It is *that they didn't see the offensive advantage of the water shaft until David saw it*. After David saw it, then they saw it. What's more, even if they couldn't see it, they didn't tell David it couldn't be done. They didn't tell him, "Joshua didn't try that and he was the baddest general Israel ever had."

Instead, when David showed them the possibility of victory the race was on. David also played on their cynicism. He challenged them to take out the "blind and lame sentries who were guarding the wall." That gives us a peek at David's sense of humor.

The first man to reach the tower was Joab, one of David's

mighty men. It should be mentioned here that the main reason Joshua couldn't take Jerusalem was because his army wasn't as strong as David's. And, as the saying goes, "the rest is history." David took Jerusalem and made it his capital city.

The next words of the narrative say, "*Then David dwelt in the stronghold, and called it the City of David.*"

Five words describe how he *captured* the city and six words describe how he *controlled* the city. *Conquest* preceded *conquering.*

New Generation people talk about what they call, "*living large,*" but they don't want to *labor long.* It's one thing to *reach the top,* but it's quite another thing to *remain at the top.*

Note that David changed the name of Jerusalem and "*called it the City of David.*"

And, you can rename your destiny today! You can change it from *failure* to success. You can change it from *losing* to *winning.*

You can rename it. Rename it *the top* instead of *the bottom.* Rename it *the first* instead of *the last.* Rename it a *soaring destiny* instead of a *struggling destiny.*

I imagine David said, "I'm changing the name of this place. From now on it's going to be called the City of David."

You can say to yourself today, "I'm changing my attitude and my achieving ability. I'm not going to be like this anymore."

You don't need to stretch out on a psychiatrist's couch and pay a hundred and fifty dollars an hour. Just stretch out on God's word! Convince yourself that you can be better and do better than you have in the past. Rename your destiny.

However, always remember *conquest* comes before *conquering.* You won't make significant achievement or improvement without a fight. And, one thing is for sure; you will have to fight against your own personal complacency. You will have to fight habitual indolence. Take David's example of achievement for your personal achievement.

The Continuous Climb

Conquering Jerusalem was only the beginning of David's success as the new King of Israel. The Bible says, "*And David went on and became great.*" Notice how many words it took to describe his first achievement. It took five words to describe David's achievement the first time, and only six words to describe his *second accomplishment*. Then it took seven words to describe his *continuous advancement*.

The higher you go the more words it will take to describe your blessed destiny. The significant factor is that David didn't start growing and becoming great when he took Jerusalem. His greatness didn't start at the top. I will prove that to you.

2 Samuel 3:1 is the record of when he was King of Judah, and it says: "*Now there was a long war between the house of Saul and the house of David. But David grew stronger and stronger.*" David grew stronger while he was King of Judah.

I was pleased when Denzel Washington received his first Academy Award as "Best Actor" *for Training Day*. However, that wasn't his first good performance. He received the Academy Award as "Best Supporting Actor" for *Glory*. He has turned in stellar performances every time they put the camera on him.

You don't get to the top and then start growing. You must grow all the way to the top and then keep on growing. No matter where fate has assigned you, you grow there. If fate has put you into a broken home, grow there. If fate has placed you with a dysfunctional family, grow there. If fate has assigned you into impoverished surroundings, grow out of there.

David didn't start growing when he became King of Israel. He was growing when he had a little kingdom down at the southern end of the country.

For people who are waiting to get a lot of money to start being generous, be warned: they won't be generous when they get a lot of money. If they're not generous with the small amount of money they have now, they won't be generous when they receive a larger amount of money later on.

Ironically, that's the main reason they won't be receiving a larger amount of money. The Lord taught us that we must be faithful with smaller amounts in order to receive larger amounts.

The account of David taking Jerusalem concludes with these words: "*And the LORD God of hosts was with him.*"

No biblical accolade or platitude ascribed to David exceeds this statement. When all of the tributes have been articulated and calculated about us, the most important thing we should want said about us is that the Lord is with us. All of David's achievement and greatness are encapsulated by those words.

The success David had in capturing Jerusalem, and his subsequent successes, brought honor to God. This statement is the explanation for his achievements as King of Israel.

The challenge for us is to let God lead us, to take on something so big that when the goal or the objective is completed everyone will know that it could only have been done because the Lord was with us.

Last, David leaves us a model of *patience, perseverance* and *progress.* His patience is shown in waiting for God to make him King; first over Judah and then over all of Israel. His perseverance is seen by the challenge to his men to take the impregnable stronghold of Jerusalem. And his progress is evidenced by the fact that he "*built all around the Millo and inward.*" He extended the kingdom further than any king who came before or after him.

RETURNING THE ARK OF THE COVENANT

Chapter Eighteen

2 Samuel 6: 1-11

Once again the Holy Spirit ushers us behind the biblical historical curtain of Israel to see another segment of David's life. And once again, through the life of David, we receive instruction and inspiration for our personal appreciation. So much can be learned from David: when he is right, wrong, weak or strong.

At the time of this episode David reigned over the United Kingdom of Israel, and the Israelites were enjoying a brief time of peace with the Philistines as well as other nations in Canaan. This time of peace allowed him the opportunity to turn his full attention from secular matters of the kingdom to spiritual matters of the kingdom. And, his heart had begun to grieve about the absence of the Ark of the Covenant from the temple, their place of worship.

Perhaps the first matter for discussion would be to answer the question, "When did Israel lose possession of the Ark?" And, that could be followed by another question: "Where had it been all the time it was out of their possession?" And, that could be followed by yet another question: "Where were they bringing the ark back from?" And, someone might even ask: "What in the world is the Ark of the Covenant?"

The history of the Ark dates all the way back to the days of Moses. It was the most sacred piece of furniture in the tabernacle. It represented the central meeting place of God and His people. The figurative meeting of God and His people was the Mercy Seat, which was the top portion, or lid, of the Ark. That was where the High Priest sprinkled the blood from the burnt offering as atonement for the sins of the people. However, it also distinctly represented the presence of God in the midst of His people. Now, of course, all of the symbolism of the Ark is fulfilled in Jesus Christ.

The Ark had been taken during the reign of King Saul. It happened after the Israelites were defeated in one of their many battles with the Philistines. Israel fled in defeat and left the Ark unguarded, so the Philistines confiscated it along with other spoils from the camp. The Holy Spirit devotes three chapters to the capture of the Ark (I Samuel 4-6).

Because of the substandard spiritual leadership of Saul, the Israelites had placed shallow, superstitious value on the presence of the Ark among them. They had adopted the custom of bringing it with them to their battles. They thought it would secure their safety, validate their victory, and prepare them for the next battle.

After the Philistines took the Ark, they displayed it in the various Philistine cities over a period of seven months. The primary reason they moved it from city to city was because the Bible particularly indicates that wherever the Ark rested in Philistine territory, "*the hand of the LORD was against that city.*"

Plagues of boils and sores were the result of it being in one Philistine city. Another city was overrun with mice. So they finally concluded that the Ark should be removed from Philistia.

Consequently, they built a new cart and placed the Ark upon it. They hitched the cart to two milk cows and chased the cows out of their territory. As the cows trotted along the countryside they finally ended up grazing in a field in Beth-Shemesh. That was how Israel took possession the Ark again. It was taken to the home of Abinadab. This is where it stayed until David returned it to the tabernacle. The Ark remained in Abinadab's house for an undisclosed length of time before David decided to bring it back to its proper place in the tabernacle.

Make mental note that there is no record that Saul ever felt the urge or the need to return the Ark to the tabernacle. And, in fact, the location of Abinadab's house was near Saul's headquarters.

Can you imagine what worship must have been like in Israel with no Ark? Where did the Priest pour the blood for the atonement after the sacrifice? Worship for them without the Ark would be like us trying to worship without using a Bible. Or, it would be like worshipping and not being unable to say the name of Jesus.

Nevertheless, the central piece for their worship had been missing an indefinitely long period of time. So the first act of spiritual enormity for David was to return the Ark back to its place in the tabernacle.

The Good Desire

It was a good desire for David to want to return the Ark to its proper place in order for it to have its proper function in worship. It's important to understand that not every well-intentioned desire is good, including the desire of service for God. Desires that may appear good on the surface can be propped up by impure motives. A person can want to serve God for his or her own self-gratification.

However, David's desire to return the Ark was genuinely good. After all, the Ark could have been returned long before he came to the throne. So there was no flaw in David's desire to return the Ark; he wanted to bring honor to the name of God by returning it to its central place.

It was a good desire. It emanated from his good heart toward God.

David felt compelled to embark on this enterprise, and his desire was based on his gratitude to God for Divine favor. It would be difficult to come up with a desire better than that! No improvement could be made upon David's desire.

Nevertheless, the good desire and pure motive David had was abdicated. God didn't honor David's good desire. It seems contradictory and sounds paradoxical, but that was what happened.

"Why?" you ask. God didn't honor David's attempt to return the Ark because it was done in grievous disobedience.

The Grievous Disobedience

Good intentions don't justify forbidden actions. You can't do a right thing the wrong way. To please God there has to be a combination of *good aim* and *good action.* David had the good aim. What he didn't have was the good action to go with it. His *desires* were offset by his *disobedience.*

As to what was so disobedient about what he attempted to do, the answer is that he violated God's direct instructions about the way the Ark should be transported. He put it on a cart.

The Philistines transported the Ark by placing it on a new cart and having it pulled by two cows, but that was not how God instructed His people move the Ark. God's people are not supposed to take their clues from the world. Paul wrote: "*Be not conformed to the world but be transformed by the renewing of your mind*" (Romans 12:2).

It appears at times that some Christian leaders think it's their responsibility to bring the church into parallel with the movement and standards of the world. It seems like a movement is on to make the church function and look like the world. However, that which is permissible by the world is not permissible in the church!

A good question is why didn't God strike down those Philistines for touching the ark and putting it on a cart? And the answer lies in the unique relationship Israel had with the Ark. Consequently, the instructions for handling and transporting the Ark were related to them in a special way. It symbolized the presence and power of God in their midst. The Ark had no significant meaning to the Philistines. Therefore, they had no responsibility for the sacred handling of the Ark. Christians, for example, are given biblical instructions, but unsaved people are not responsible for heeding those instructions. When there is no *relationship with God, neither is there any responsibility to God.* Worldly people are not bound to the Word.

The instructions for handling and hauling the Ark weren't given to the Philistines; they were given to God's people. Therefore, *the grievous disobedience* I speak of was the way David attempted to transport the Ark. He attempted to transport it in the same manner as the Philistines did, putting it on a new cart and having it pulled by oxen. But, it wouldn't have mattered if they had put it on an old cart or some other conveyance, simply because it was not the way God instructed them to transport the Ark.

As to the proper way to transport the Ark, the instructions are in Exodus 25 and Numbers 4. After God gave Moses directions about the construction of the Ark, He followed with directions for transporting it. "*And you shall cast four rings of gold for it and put them in the four corners, two rings shall be on one side.*" And more instructions followed: "*You shall make staves of acacia wood and overlay them with gold and you shall put the staves into the rings by the side of the Ark that the Ark may be borne with them.*"

David's disobedience was three-fold. He disregarded the *method*, the *mode*, and the *manner* for the way the ark was to be transported. It was to be *lifted* with staves, handled by sanctified men. It was supposed to be loaded on the shoulders of sanctified men and it was supposed to be *launched* forward by sanctified men.

We should always be careful to note when God is being gender specific. When God has a task for a man, God wants a man for that task. And when God has a task for a woman, God wants a woman for that task.

Furthermore, the instructions for transporting the Ark were given to the Levites. The Levites were the priests. That means handling the Ark was restricted to men in the tribe of Levi, not men in general. An additional restriction was that not every Levite could handle the Ark. Men in general, and Levites in general, couldn't just pick up the Ark and walk off with it. Only particular men among the Levites were assigned the task of *caring* for and *carrying* the Ark.

In the time of Moses there were nearly one thousand Levites in the camp, but not all of them could take care of the Ark. Only the sons of Kohath had that responsibility (Numbers 4:4). We only need to know the distinction between a son and a daughter, a girl and a boy, and a man and a woman, to follow God's instructions concerning the Ark. However, even the sons of Kohath couldn't touch the Ark. They could only lift it *with* staves.

Consequently, there was a restrictive line drawn for what they could do. These distinctive restrictions and instructions for handling the Ark help us see the *grievous disobedience* of David.

In total disregard to God's instructions for moving the Ark, they put it on a new cart and had it pulled by oxen. However, when they reached Nacon's threshing floor with it, the oxen stumbled and the Ark shook. Actually it began to teeter and totter back and forth on the cart to the point where it looked as if it was going to fall to the ground for sure. And to keep it from falling, a man named Uzzah reached out his hand to balance and steady the Ark. Then came the solemn words: "*God struck him there for his error, and there he died by the Ark of God.*"

In the words of the olden preachers, he was "graveyard dead." God is serious about what he wants done, whom he wants to do it, and how he wants it done. One look at Uzzah and you will see He is dead serious.

The apparent harshness of God often draws criticism from some theologians and well-meaning Christians. Their conclusion is that Uzzah reacted in innocence. However, he wasn't acting in *innocence*, but in *ignorance*. There is a difference between an innocent act and an ignorant act.

The fullest extent of innocence isn't the *not knowing* something is wrong, but also is when a person *can't know* something is wrong. Children too small to know the consequences of their actions have, unknowingly, committed atrocious actions. An ignorant act is when a person *could have known or, more importantly, should have known*.

The root word for ignorant comes from the word "ignore." As a Levite, Uzzah could have informed the King about the proper way to move the Ark. Some people feel as if it was David's fault, and it was – but he was not totally at fault. Blame can be divided equally between them.

As strange as it seems, the Bible says, "*David was displeased because the LORD had broken forth in anger against Uzzah*." It's a typical reaction that when we walk in disobedience to the will of God, we are displeased when God corrects us. David was angry with God but, thank goodness, he made a quick adjustment. It was a fast mood swing. He went from *fuming at God* to *fearing God* in a very brief time. After indicating that David was displeased with God, the Bible says, "*and David was afraid of the LORD that day, and said, 'How shall the Ark come to me?*'"

The English translation falters by saying David was afraid of the LORD. The Hebrew word that is translated to mean "afraid" is "rever," from which we get reverence. It was *reverential fear*, not "knee-knocking" fear. Nevertheless, the project of moving the Ark back to Jerusalem was put on hold. It was, instead, taken to the home of a man named Obed-Edom, where it remained for three months. However, the house of Obed-Edom was blessed because of the presence of the Ark. The blessings that were upon his house were in perfect consistency with the presence of the Ark. The Ark was not intended to cause death; it symbolized life. It was supposed to be a blessing to the people of God, not a curse.

Therefore, when David heard that Obed-Edom's house was being blessed because of the presence of the Ark, he took it to mean that he could resume the project of bringing it back to Jerusalem. David's quandary, however, was how to get it moved to Jerusalem. After all, no one could touch it. David had apparently taken reflective thought about what had happened when the Ark was placed on the cart. He must also have done due diligence to find out the proper way to transport the Ark.

This is indicated by 1 Chronicles 15:2, the companion narrative. "*Then David said, 'None ought to carry the Ark of God but the Levites; for them has the LORD chosen to carry THE ARK OF GOD, and to minister unto Him forever.*" And David called priests Zadok and Abiathar to lead the procession, and several Levites to attend to the Ark. He shared these words before the procession began: "*For because you did it not at the first, the LORD our God broke forth upon us, because we sought Him not in the proper way.*"

Perhaps it was through personal meditation and soul searching that David received inspiration from God regarding how the Ark should be transported.

The Grateful Delight

David was, obviously, delighted to hear that the presence of the Ark had blessed the house of Obed-Edom. This news encouraged him to resume the task of moving the Ark to Jerusalem. Nevertheless, after the procession had gone only six paces, he ordered them to stop and he sacrificed seven oxen and seven rams.

These sacrifices were to sanctify the people who made up the procession. It equates to the consecration that Christians should do before corporate worship. There should be a pause for a moment of consecration before corporate worship begins.

When the consecration was finished, David blessed the people and gave the signal for the procession to start up again. David positioned himself in front of the procession and then the Bible says, "*and David danced before the LORD.*"

His dancing was an exhibition of *grateful delight*. Who more than David had reason to be the most exuberant among those in the procession? The Lord told a parable about gratitude, and the conclusion was that the person who had been forgiven the most should be the most grateful. He also said, "*To whom much is given, much is required.*" So David was the most exuberant, the most enthusiastic, and the most excited of all the worshippers in the processional.

David wrote eleven psalms about this processional! Perhaps the favorite of them all is Psalm 24: "*Lift up your head, oh ye gates. And even lift them up ye everlasting doors, and the King of Glory shall come in.*" The personification of the King of Glory was the presence of the Ark. Nevertheless, David's wife Mical came out to meet him and condemned him for dancing in what she considered was an indecent manner. With scorn and sarcasm she said, "*You sure were glorious today, O King.*" She publicly berated him.

No one can diffuse worship enthusiasm like a family member. For many Christians, the worse time of their worship day is when they have to return home to an insensitive spouse, or a critical loved one who does not know beans about God, His grace and His mercy.

David, however, wouldn't allow his enthusiastic worship to be diffused. His response to his disgusted wife essentially conveyed the thought that he could, and would, become even more "undignified" in his celebration, considering how good and gracious the Lord had been to him. He told her: "*I will be even more undignified than this, and will be humble in my own sight.*" And, from that day forth, David did not consider Mical to be his wife.

The main application for us from this narrative is to be sure that our plan and goals for service to God match His will, His Word, and His way. We must make sure that *our will* to do service matches *the way* the Lord wants it done.

In this story David also gives us a model of how to correct a mistake. He sought instructions from the Word of God as to how the Ark was to be moved. We can avoid the tragic error David committed simply by referring to the Word of God for what God has said. Simply put, let God's Word be the structure for your lifestyle. Agree with God's Word even if you do not understand it. Once David discovered the way the Ark was to be moved, it was "smooth sailing" all the way to Jerusalem. It's an example of the confusions and frustrations we can avoid by relying on the Word of God. This is another case where David provides us a life-size example of trust and obedience.

WHEN GOD SAID "NO" TO DAVID

Chapter Nineteen

2 Samuel 7: 1-16

Once again an episode from the life of David provides us inspiration and information for personal application. David's life is far more than an ancient story from years past. It is replete with lessons for our Christian enrichment. It fulfills the meaning of Paul's words in 2 Timothy 3:16 that "*all Scripture is given by inspiration of God and is profitable for doctrine, for reproof, for correction and for instruction in righteousness.*"

And, invaluable lessons can be gleaned from the time when God said "no" to David.

A sure way of evaluating and determining Christian maturity is when God tells us "no." It measures the genuineness of our relationship with God, and the depth of our faith in God. Of course, we have to admit that we don't like it when God tells us "no."

The experience clashes with the viewpoint known as "name it and claim it" that falsely implies that God will always say "yes." That viewpoint is a long stretch when it comes to our attempts to always get a "yes" from God. In John 14:13 the Lord says, "*And whatever you ask in My name, that will I do, that the Father may be glorified in the Son.*"

The part the so-called "faith and prosperity preachers" like to emphasize is "whatever you ask, that I will do." The problem is that they leave out "that the Father may be glorified in the Son." This means that what we ask for should bring glory to God. Unfortunately, much of what we pray for *is not* for *God's glory* but for *our greed.*

There is absolute certainty that God will, and does, say "no" sometimes. God's answer to our prayers is based on sovereign omniscience. God knows the purity of our motives, and whether we have the maturity to handle the blessing we are asking for; consequently, whatever His answer is what is best for us.

We must recognize it's God's will when the answer is "no" just as it is when He says "yes." We must not only recognize God's will when He *supplies blessings*, but also recognize His will when He *suspends blessings*. We must recognize His will when He *presents blessings*, but we must also recognize His will when He *prevents blessings.*

This is why Job's historic testimony is so rich in the content of his maturity. After God had taken away his *family* and *fortune* he said, "*The Lord has given and the Lord has taken away, blessed be the name of the Lord.*" He was content with God's right to say "no" or "yes." Every Christian has had the experience of wanting to do something where God said "no."

It reminds me of the story of a man who announced his call to preach. After he preached his first sermon, he dropped out of sight and wasn't seen for months. Finally, one day a sister from the church saw him downtown in a place of ill repute and confronted him about his call to preach. He politely responded to her and said, "My dear sister, God did call me to preach, but after He heard me, He told me 'never mind.'"

The essence of this narrative conveys clearly and simply that sometimes God does say "no," which is His prerogative. However, it's not an arbitrary prerogative. God doesn't say "no" to spite or punish us.

It's also important to think about the fact that we usually reject God's answer when it is "no" and, if we don't *reject it*, we at least *resent it*. However, with the passing of time and the coming of more maturity, we eventually come to appreciate the times when God has said "no" to us.

It's important that our dreams, desires, and goals don't impose on God's will for our life. After all, sometimes *our* voice sounds just like *God's* voice, especially when we're talking to ourselves. We can convince ourselves to think that the voice we are hearing is God's voice.

Still fresh in my memory is the time a young lady informed me that God had consented for her to marry a man who was not saved. Nothing I could say, or show her in Scripture, would convince her that what she was saying meant God was essentially contradicting Himself. The Word forbids us to be unequally yoked. She insisted that she was right and married the guy, and it didn't last eighteen months. The point is that sometimes we can psyche ourselves into believing that we have heard God say "yes" when, in fact, He has said "no."

The Resolve

David's resolve to build a temple for God flowed out of his resolve to return the Ark to the tabernacle. Returning the Ark was the first spiritual act initiated by David as King of Israel. However, there were also other activities he exercised leadership over as King of Israel that were spiritual in nature. Notwithstanding, his resolve to build a house of worship for God may be considered the second item on his agenda of spiritual acts. "*Now it came to pass when the king was dwelling in his house, and the LORD had given him rest from all his enemies all around, that the king said to Nathan the prophet, 'See now, I dwell in a house of cedar, but The Ark of God dwells inside tent curtains.'*"

These verses are chocked full of spiritual content. There David was enjoying rest God had given him from battle engagements with his enemies (our modern vernacular would describe him as "living large"), yet his spiritual sensitivity is seen in his desire to build a house for God. His house of cedar took seven years to build, and we should note what a sharp contrast living as king was compared to when he was living in caves and sleeping in the woods while running for Saul. Nevertheless, he was embarrassed that there was no house for God. This indicates his desire wasn't a whimsical resolve. Neither was it a careless wish. He *was content* with what God had done for him, but he was *not content* with what he had done for God. Despite his luxurious lifestyle, he still looked for ways in which he could honor God. So his resolve to build God a house came from his reflection on the goodness of God.

The Refusal

The Bible says God told Nathan, "*Go tell my servant David that he shall not build Me a house.*"

God told David "no."

I alluded to earlier, the fact that one of the most difficult times in a Christian's life is when he or she has to deal with a refusal from God. It's a good test of our genuine spirituality.

Paul told the church in Corinth, "*Don't be like children in understanding.*" Many times, if not most of the time, we act like children when God tells us "no." However, all parents know that good parenting requires telling children "no." Every parent knows what it is like to take something away from a child that is potentially dangerous. And, we have experienced the selfish and senseless response of the child, which is exactly how some Christians act when God tells them "no."

I wanted to go to college straight from high school, but the Lord said "no. Furthermore, when I finally enrolled in college I wanted to be a lawyer, and once again God said "no." When I chose my first church in Fresno, California, the Lord said "no." When I wanted to marry my first love, the Lord said "no." (I fell hard in love in junior high school, but at my twenty-fifth high school reunion, the Lord let me see that girl, and my soul and spirit did "high-fives" in my bosom as I praised God for His omniscient wisdom). I remembered my grandmother's teaching that it is always wise to let the Lord have His way.

It's not only our responsibility to recognize God's will when He says "yes," we are also responsible for recognizing God's will when He says "no." We must agree with God when He bestows blessings as well as when He blocks blessings.

A simple fact to remember is God sees the total picture when He says "no." and we don't. That's why He says "no." God isn't looking at the result from an angle, either from the left or the right. God has total vision, not tunnel vision.

The Reason

God doesn't arbitrarily say "no," just as He doesn't arbitrarily say "yes." God isn't being mean or vindictive, nor is He punishing us when He says "no." Granted, sometimes God says "no" as a consequence of our behavior. And, sometimes God says "no" because of our lack of faith.

In David's case the reason was two-fold. First, it was because of *facts* about God. God reminded David that He had never dwelt in a house since Israel was brought up out of Egypt. God had not required that the King of Israel should build Him as house.

So a good idea may not be God's idea.

David had a good idea, but it wasn't God's idea. Specifically, it wasn't God's idea for David to build the house. Another reason why God refused to let David build the house was because his hands were stained with blood. That, however, wasn't revealed to David until later. It is mentioned in 1 Chronicles

22:8. It appears that God allowed David some maturing time before He told him about his hands being stained with blood. Consequently, because of certain facts about God, David was forbidden to build God a house.

A second reason for the refusal was because of the *future* of David. When God tells us "no," He does it because of facts relating to our future. Don't forget that God sees the total picture of our lives. God forbade David to build a house because God *was* going to build David a house.

Nathan relayed God's intention to build David a house. Not a house of bricks and mortar, granite and stone, but a house of posterity. God's house for David was to "establish the throne of his kingdom forever." *Remember, when Jesus came, He was of the house of David.* Ultimately the reason for the refusal was because God had plans to honor David in the same way David had wanted to honor God.

The Reaction

David's reaction was revealed in these words: "*Then went King David in and sat before the Lord.*"

This was a totally different reaction compared to David's reaction when Uzzah touched the Ark, when he was displeased with the Lord. Apparently some degree of maturity had taken place in David between Chapter 6 when Uzzah touched the Ark and Chapter 7 when he received word from Nathan that he couldn't build God a house.

This is obvious by his reaction. To sit before the Lord doesn't refer to his physical posture, but rather to his spiritual posture. The Hebrew word that is translated "sat" is ya'shab. It means *reflection* or *meditation*. This suggests that we are to sit before the Lord when we don't know what God is doing in our lives. It's an example of what to do when God tells us "no" about something we want to do.

No doubt, David went to the tabernacle. This may be the background experience for David's inspiration to write Psalm 46: "*Be still and know that I am God.*" David probably sat there in reverence, but possibly also in astonishment and said: "*And yet this was a small thing in your sight, O Lord God; and you have also spoken of your servant's house for a great while to come. Is this the manner of man, O Lord God?*"

The better translation would be "*This is not the manner of men.*" This is not how it is done in corporate America. This is not how it is done in the private sector. Furthermore, it can also be said that this is not how it is done sometimes even in the church.

David's reaction and receptivity to God's refusal ending words of verse 20, "*for you Lord, know your servant.*" When God tells us "no," or forbids us to go in a certain direction, or puts our blessing on hold, we ought to be able to say, "*Lord, you know your servant.*" Instead of throwing a conniption fit and rolling around on the floor like a spoiled brat, we should realize that God knows us. That is, He knows what's best for us.

When our paychecks are irregular the proper response is "*Lord you know.*" When it looks like there is no certainty in the direction of our life, the proper response is "*Lord you know.*"

An unchallengeable certainty is that God knows us. God knows what we can take and what we can't take. God knows what blessings will help us and what blessings will hurt us. When God's reply is "no" our response should be "yes." Not "yes" against God's will, but "yes" to affirm God's will. Not "yes" in conflict with God's will, but "yes" to confirm God's will. Not "yes" in defiance of God's will, but "yes" in deference to God's will. We must accept and realize that God knows what's best for us. The old song's lyrics are: "*We are our Heavenly Father's children and He loves us one and all, and He knows, yes He knows, just how much we can bear.*"

The Holy Spirit has this truth laying right out there on the surface of this narrative, and if you're not careful you will miss it: *when God says "no," He has something better for you later on.*

David wanted to build God a house and God said, "Oh, no, I'm going to build you a house."

Young people, you shouldn't grieve because of a breakup with a boyfriend or a girlfriend. Instead of *grieving* you ought to be *grinning!* It means God has someone better for you later on.

God told David "no" and then informed him that He was going to build him a house. Furthermore, the house that God intended to build for David meant more to him than the house he was going to build for God.

David provides a good example of what to do and how to react when God says "no." However, he's not the best example. But, for the best example we must look past David to the Son of David. When Jesus had prayed in the Garden of Gethsemane three agonizing times for an alternative to going to Calvary, and was denied each time, He then said, "*Not My will but Your will be done.*"

And because of His willingness to go to the cross, God has made Jesus both Lord and Christ, and has given Him a name above every name. God's will is always better than our will, and God's way is always better than our way.

When God says "no" He has something better for us than we can possibly imagine. The lyrics of old hymn put it succinctly:

Thy way, O Lord, not mine
Thy will be done, not mine
Incline my heart each day
To say, thy will be done.

GRACE FOR MEPHIBOSHETH

Chapter Twenty

2 Samuel 9: 1-13

The evidence of David's spiritual quality is displayed over and over again through the various experiences of his life. The caring and tender way he treated Mephibosheth is a graphic example of his inner spiritual quality. Make no mistake about it, who we really are underneath will come to the surface through the various occurrences of our lives. The swift shifting transitions of life will reveal our strengths, weaknesses, and the good, the bad, and the ugly.

For example, having a *little substance*, or a *lot of substance*, will expose us for who we really are underneath. Some people don't do well with a little substance, and they certainly wouldn't do well with a whole lot of substance. Some people have the propensity to forget how things were when they had only a little, and when they get a lot they become selfish, smug, and live self-centered lives.

But not David!

David didn't forget Who his blessings had come from. All of the years of running from Saul taught him the invaluable lessons of the necessitude of life.

Please notice that 2 Samuel 8 sets up chapter 9. The Holy Ghost knows how to write a script in the same way as a playwright. He knows how to build, transition, one chapter to the next. 2 Samuel 8 shows us the extensive expansion of David's kingdom. The border of it stretched all the way to Moab and extended to the Euphrates River. He set garrisons of soldiers in the occupied territories in the same sense that our country has a military presence all over the world.

Our Navy is docked in foreign ports, and we've got embassies hither there and yon, and David's kingdom was essentially as progressive and prosperous as our nation is today. The conquered kings paid tribute money to him. The Moabites and the Syrians became David's servants and brought him gifts. Joram brought with him "*vessels of silver and vessels of gold and vessels of bronze.*" However, David didn't use any of the tribute money or treasure to personally enrich himself. "*King David also dedicated these to the LORD, along with the silver and the gold that he had dedicated from all the nations, which he had subdued.*"

This means David was a settled, sustained, respected, revered, and rich ruler. His mind wasn't on what he was *going to achieve* but whom *he was going to assist*. His agenda wasn't about what he was going to take over but whom he was going to take in. Unlike Alexander the Great, who sat in his tent and wept like a spoiled brat when there were no more armies to fight and no more lands to conquer, David's mind was not on getting, but on giving.

The Uncommon Attitude

David apparently called a staff meeting of his leaders one day and inquired, "*Is there still anyone who is left of the house of Saul, that I may show him kindness for Jonathan's sake.*" This was an uncommon attitude, asking if there were anyone in the household of Saul whom he could bless.

He called in his advisors, counselors, and department heads. These leaders no doubt came in expecting to engage in a deep, mind-stretching, military exercise to expand the kingdom. They would likely have come thinking they were going to discuss foreign policy, domestic state or what would be the next military target. Instead, however, David asked if there were anyone from Saul's household whom he could bless.

This was an uncommon attitude because what was common in David's time was for the new king to destroy all the descendants of the previous king. So what was especially uncommon was not only David wanting to show kindness, but to whom he wanted to show that kindness.

Don't miss it. The question wasn't, "Is there anyone worthy?" Or, "Is there anyone qualified?" The question wasn't "Is there anyone educated enough?" Or, "Is there anyone who is good enough?" The question was simply, "*Is there anyone of the household of Saul whom I can bless for Jonathan's sake*?"

The designation of "anyone" makes it not only an uncommon inquiry, but an inclusive inquiry as well. Earlier we saw where David made a covenant with Jonathan that he would keep Jonathan's descendants alive. Nevertheless, David's inquiry was beyond the perimeters of his covenant with Jonathan. He enlarged the borders of the covenant to include anyone of the household of Saul. The indication is if there were no descendants of Jonathan, or in addition to Jonathan's descendants, he would bless any descendants of Saul as well. David's attitude was right in line with a hymn with the lyrics: "*If I can help somebody, as I pass along, if I can cheer somebody with a word or song, then my living shall not be in vain.*"

When it comes to the recognition of achievements in a lifetime, we must include those we have helped. The question shouldn't be, "What do I have?" but rather, "Who have I helped?" It isn't about who you are, but about whom you have helped.

The common way of determining wealth and prestige is to count up how much a person has done for himself or herself. That's the American way to determine wealth. Episodes of the *Lifestyles of the Rich and Famous* always calculate wealth by how many houses the people featured built or bought for *themselves*, how many cars they have for *themselves*, and how many boats they have for *themselves*? But when we calculate wealth from a Christian perspective, it's how many and whom we have helped. Who have you helped, or whom are you helping?

And, no one other than you needs to know about the person, or people, you help. You shouldn't be keeping a tab, or a score. But, who will be able to point to you years from now and say, "If it hadn't been for him (or her), I would not have made it." I'm not talking about loaning someone ten dollars; I'm talking about giving someone a thousand dollars without expecting anything in return. Who have you helped? Every Christian should be able to recall names of people we have helped. And it is equally important to remember those who have helped us. I have a long roll call of people who have helped me.

David shows us again that he has a heart like God's heart, which is why he was a man after God's own heart. David did what God does. God searches in and around project apartments in the inner city and raises up men and women for His glory. God goes into prison cells and changes minds and reconstructs attitudes to find souls who will proclaim His name. To bless people, God looks in the backcountry, way back in the woods somewhere, which is where He found me.

Jesus epitomized the nature of God in helping the down and out, the downtrodden and disenfranchised. He hung out and around people of low estate, and when He was criticized for the company He kept, He said, "*I am not come to call the righteous, but the sinners to repentance*." So the attitude that David displayed was, indeed, an uncommon one.

The Unusual Approach

The response to David's question came immediately. One of his leaders responded, with news that there was a servant of the house of Saul whose name was Ziba. So David had Ziba brought in before him. If we put an "e" in the place of the "I," and insert an "r" between the "b" and the "a," his name would be Zebra. And that name is a closer representation of his character, which comes clearer by some of his actions later on in the narrative.

We should make the distinction between the "uncommon attitude" and the "unusual approach." Mental attitude was followed by manifested action. Attitude is *thinking* but approach is *tangible*. Attitude is *internal*, but approach is *external*. It is one thing to say you are going to do something, but quite a different thing when the time comes to do it.

It's common to talk oneself out of doing something between the *attitude* that *conceives* the idea and the *action* that *completes* the idea. We can easily talk ourselves out of helping someone by finding a flaw in the character of the person. The conclusion is that the person is unworthy and wouldn't appreciate what we were planning to do anyway. The ironic certainty is the small chance of you finding someone who is unworthy. However, David didn't talk himself out of his good intention to help someone. Furthermore, neither did he allow anyone else to talk him out of it.

There was no lag time, no hang time, no hesitation time between the *intention* and the *implementation*. David sent his leaders out to find Ziba. When Ziba was brought before him, David asked, "*Is there anyone of the household of Saul whom I can show the kindness of God?*" David wasn't offering *his* kindness; he was offering *God's* kindness. The secret to David's action is to be willing to do what God wants done the way God wants it done. It's not the amount you want to give; it's the amount that God wants you to give. It's about showing God's kindness.

No one could do much with your kindness. If someone really needed help, he or she couldn't do much with our generosity. The clarification is this it's not about what David wanted to do; it's about what God wanted him to do. It wasn't David's compassion that was motivating him; it was God's compassion. Neither, was David's generosity on display in this story; it was God's generosity being fleshed out in David's character.

Nevertheless, when Ziba stood before David, he was delighted to inform him that there was a descendant of Jonathan alive whose name was Mephibosheth. He supplied additional information, particularly, that the son was lame in his feet and where he lived.

The Unprecedented Action

David's benevolent and gracious movement went from *attitude*, to *approach*, and then to *action*. He took the next step and sent for Mephibosheth. When Ziba spoke of Mephibosheth, he also described his physical condition: "But he's lame in his feet." Knowing the background and bias of the Jewish culture toward cripples helps to shed light on the meaning of Ziba's statement.

Jews typically looked upon crippled people with utter disdain. Their crippled physical condition was thought to be an act of God, specifically a punishment from God for some sin they were presumed to have committed. This was the background to the question the disciples asked Jesus about the man who was born blind. They asked, "*Master, who did sin, this man or his parents that he is born blind*?" Their thinking and theology influenced their question. And the Lord's explanation was that his condition was not related to anyone's sin.

However, because of this falsely preconceived view that cripples were being punished for sin, Jews treated cripples harshly – the equivalent of how they might treat a dog. The truth of why Mephibosheth was crippled was because his nurse had dropped him on his feet while was a young child.

It happened the day that Saul and Jonathan were killed. His nurse presumed he was the next in line to be king and would be the homicidal target of the new king. In her attempt to run with him in her arms to a secret hiding place, she stumbled, dropped him, and injured his feet.

David, however, gave no response to the physical description of Mephibosheth. His next question was, "Where is he?" He didn't ask, "How bad is his handicap? Can he walk at all? When did it happen? How did it happen? Where did it happen?" He didn't ask, "Was he born like that?" All David wanted to know was, "Where is he?"

David's persistence in finding Mephibosheth is a personified description of the grace of God. This was a demonstration of love undeserved and unearned. It is commonly called unmerited favor.

Mephibosheth lived in Lo-debar. The prefix "Lo" means "no," and "debar," means "pastureland." He was living in a place of no pastureland. Lo-debar was the most barren area in all Israel. However, people lived in Lo-debar either by choice or by circumstance. Lo-debar was a place for social outcasts. Lo-debar was where people of low self-esteem resided. If a person wanted to hide, and live incognito, Lo-debar was the place to go. Usually no one bothered to go that far out of the way to find some one. So there is spiritual, emotional, and economical significance to this place called Lo-debar.

Many people live in a Lo-debar-like environment. However, people live in such an environment by choice or by circumstance. Nevertheless, in either case they can relocate from there by an act of the will. The reason I know is because I'm acquainted with Lo-debar conditions. I was born in Lo-debar conditions and I had to deal with a system that was set up to keep me in those conditions, but I made a choice to move when I accepted Christ as my savior. Education is suggested as the means of getting people out of "Lo-debar conditions," and it is important. But, it's not *education* first; it's *salvation* first.

With the help of imagination, we can conclude that an emissary of the King, with a summons from the King, was the last visitor that Mephibosheth wanted to see. That's why he was living in Lo-debar. He thought he was on David's hit list. This is evidenced by the humbled way he came before David. He stood there as a surrendered foe, ready to accept his fate. In his mind David was his enemy, but in David's mind he was a friend.

I had a situation similar to this some time ago when I, quite unexpectedly, met up with a man who owed me some money. It was apparent by his actions that I was the last person he wanted to see that day. He looked as if he had seen a ghost. Because he had owed me for such a long time, he was fidgety and tense when I struck up a conversation – until he realized that I wasn't going to mention the money. Then he relaxed and started talking and joking and *slapping me on the back, but I haven't forgotten.* We ended the conversation and went our separate ways, and he probably thinks he has gotten away with not paying back the money, but he hasn't. I have a Heavenly Father who takes care of folks who mistreat me. I don't have to go tracking, or packing, behind anyone who has mistreated me; my Heavenly Fathers watches over me.

Nevertheless, Mephibosheth came in before David trembling and thinking that he was going to meet his fate. There are some sociological elements at work in this meeting. He had one thing in his mind and David had something else in his mind. He was thinking the worse was going to happen to him and David was thinking the best was going to happen to him.

Sometimes people will misjudge you with no evidence at all. Sometimes their not liking you is nothing more than a whim or misconception about who you are. David disarmed Mephibosheth with his gracious offer to restore to him all the land Saul had owned, to hire servants to tend his fields and vineyards, and then invited him to be a permanent guest at the King's table. David left Mephibosheth *disarmed, diffused* and *dumbfounded.* When he was able to speak he bowed himself and said, "*What is your servant that you should look upon such a dead dog as I*?"

A dog, as previously mentioned, was the characteristic Jewish description of a cripple, and Mephibosheth embellished that description even more by referring to himself as a "dead dog." The answer to his question, of course, is that's the way grace works. Grace is exclusively for the undeserving. Not only did David exhibit an *uncommon attitude*, an *unusual approach*, and an *unprecedented action*, there was also an *unmerited adoption*. Mephibosheth's place at David's table would be in the family section. The invitation specifically said, "*As for Mephibosheth, he shall eat at my table like one of the King's sons.*"

This old story epitomizes the *manifestation, movement, measure, and materialization* of God's grace. The invitation to Mephibosheth to eat at David's table is mentioned four times. Whenever God repeats something four times in one chapter, it has to be significant. It was, no doubt, such an unusual invitation that Mephibosheth had to hear it four times for it to sink in. Furthermore, it is repeated in the closing lines of the narrative with the words, "*and he was lame in both feet.*"

The Holy Spirit attaches those words to drive home the main point of this story: *that grace is never merited.* Mephibosheth never stopped being lame. The spiritual comparison is that we never become worthy of God's grace. Just as Mephibosheth's physical condition never improved, our spiritual condition never improves. Our relationship *starts* with God's grace, and it's *sustained* by God's grace. No wonder it's called *Amazing Grace.*

DAVID AND BATHSHEBA

Chapter Twenty-One

2 Samuel 11:1-17

The Word of God doesn't conceal the flaws of even the Lord's greatest servants. Noah's drunkenness is recorded in God's book, as is Abraham's lies and infidelity. Jacob's trickery is recorded in God's book, as is Moses' explosive anger that resulted in the murder of the Egyptian taskmaster. Peter's cussing and cutting is recorded in God's book. Saul (Paul) reprehensibly persecuted the church, and it's recorded in God's book.

The list goes on and on, so it rightfully includes King David's transgressions. David's infidelity, and the murder he initiated to cover it up, is also recorded in God's book. Actually, and ironically, this is one of the main proofs of the credibility of the Word of God – *nothing is left out*. It tells it like it is.

However, we write our life stories differently than God does. For example, if I wrote my life story, I guarantee that there would be some things I wouldn't include. And, I'm bold enough to suggest that you would do the same. God, however, does not edit, or revise, anything – including the bad stuff – about the men and women of the Bible. The flaws, the weaknesses, the misbehavior; it's all included. When God writes a life story it comes with "warts and all" warning label. This is even true of "*the man after God's own heart.*"

In previous chapters we may have discovered things that were unknown to us about David, but few people, whether Christian or non-Christian, haven't heard the story of *David and Bathsheba.* Many of the good and noble things David did are not commonly known, but his affair with Bathsheba is well known. The words spoken by Marc Antony, when he eulogized Julius Caesar, are true: "*The bad that men do lives on after them but the good is interred with their bones.*" That's true of David, and it's true of you and me. People will remember the worst about us long after they have *forgotten the best* about us.

In my Bible there is an inscription prefacing 2 Samuel 11. It reads: "*David's Great Sin.*" By implication it suggests the other sins of David were not as great as this sin. But, please understand that the Holy Spirit did not write the inscription. Bible translators took the liberty of putting it there.

Those words are not inspired.

However, they suggest how easy it is to compare so-called "small" sins with "big" sins. The Word of God clearly states, "*All unrighteousness is sin.*" Furthermore, the requirement for forgiveness of adultery is the same as the requirement for forgiveness of every other sin. "*If we confess our sins He is faithful and just to forgive us our sins, and will cleanse us from all unrighteousness.*"

The truth of this narrative lies right on the surface. We don't have to *be let down into the deep treasure of God's Word* to discover the truth. We don't need the technique of *inductive* exegesis and *deductive* exegesis for this story. There is nothing that we have to dig for. It's *impartially* clear and *immanently* graphic.

The Foul Up

One evening David took what was intended to be a relaxing stroll across the rooftop of his palace. Maybe he wanted to view the aesthetic beauty of a sunset or, perhaps, it was for exercise to relieve himself of the stresses, pressure, and responsibility of being king over such a vast kingdom. Whatever the reason, as he was walking he saw a gorgeous woman taking a bath. The Hebrew word *raw-aw* is translated "*saw.*" But, the word has various dimensions and derivative meanings. In this case it meant "*gaze*" or "stare." Sometimes the meaning is "consider." For David, it was all of the above. *He saw, gazed, stared*, and *considered*. He was seized with desire.

To avoid the long-standing debate about who should bear the blame for the illicit relationship that followed, it is fair to agree that the blame can be equally divided between David and Bathsheba. Women are taught about modesty when they are girls. Men, on the other hand, have the instinctive nature of being aroused by sight. Between those two behaviors blame can be placed on both the King and the woman. There is the opinion, however, that indicates Bathsheba was taken advantage of because David was in a position of authority over her. The explanation is she couldn't resist the king because of the authority that he had over her.

The record, of course, does not indicate that she offered any resistance. If the conclusion is that she *couldn't* have resisted because he was the King, there is a story in the Book of Esther about another woman named Vashti who refused the inappropriate suggestions of a king. The fact is that both David and Bathsheba can lay claim to the blame for what happened.

This leads into the matter of harassment. My intention is never to belittle or demean the occasion of genuine sexual harassment. It's unacceptable behavior, period. However, harassment runs along a two-way street. Some sisters in church are capable of a little bit of harassment on their own. Some of our single guys say they start putting on the whole armor of God when they turn the corner and start coming up the hill to the church. Some sisters in the church know how to put the pressure on a brother! Sexual harassment can never be justified, and in every case it is unacceptable behavior. But, it's also unacceptable for a lady to consent and then later on to become vindictive and claim she consented because she felt threatened. It's not harassment unless what is being said or done is offensive to the other person. A woman shouldn't flirt back and give the appearance that she enjoys what is being said or done if she wants to avoid harassment. Don't go to lunch with the man if you know his intentions are immoral. Seek the wisdom of God for what you should say and not say, and for what you should do and not do.

Any illicit sexual relationship will eventually come to an end. Any man or any woman needs to know that from the outset. The reason is because it has no foundation. So when it comes to an end, pick up the pieces of your emotions off the floor and continue on with your life. Hey bro, when it's over, don't be stalking the sister. Don't show up in the parking lot at work or peek in the windows at her house. It's over, man!

Sister girl, you shouldn't hold a man hostage and extort money from him. It's over now. Maybe he became interested in someone else, or maybe you became interested in someone else. Whatever the reason, it's over. It *didn't last* because it *couldn't last.* These kinds of relationships never have lasting duration; they will eventually end. If you can't *contemplate the ending*, don't *consummate the beginning*. Like they say, if you can't do the time, don't do the crime.

"*From his roof he saw a woman bathing, and the woman was very beautiful to behold.*" That reminds me of the old preacher who was preaching about lust and adultery, and he was taking the King James Version literally. He said, "The Bible don't say you can't look. You can look all you want to look and look as long as you want to look. Looking is not a sin. The Bible says when you *looketh* on a woman with lust in your heart you have sinned. You can look all you want to, but don't *looketh*. When you *looketh*, that's when you sin." His simple exaggeration is humorous, but dangerously in error.

The image of David staring at Bathsheba reminds me of a song entitled, *Welcome to the Hotel California*. It starts off, "I saw her standing in the door when I pulled into the driveway as I heard the mission bell, and I said to myself this could be heaven or this could be hell."

And the last words of the song are, "Welcome to Hotel California, you can check out, but you can't leave." There's a connection to the guy, the song, and David that is familiar.

The sequence of *The Foul Up* started with *looking*, which was followed by *liking* what he saw, which was followed by *lusting* for what he saw, which was followed by *losing* resistance. However, resistance wasn't all David lost. James 1:14-15 says, "*But each one is tempted when he is drawn away by his own desires and enticed. Then, when desire has conceived, it gives birth to sin; and sin, when it is full-grown, brings forth death.*"

David sent for her, she consented, and *she conceived*. The worst result imaginable happened; Bathsheba became pregnant. Under the right circumstances, when a woman discovers she is pregnant it's supposed to be a blessing, not a burden. When a woman discovers she's pregnant it's supposed to be a happy, not a horrific, occasion. However, this was not happy news for either of them. David did essentially what Adam and Eve did when they tried to cover themselves with fig leaves after sinning in the Garden of Eden. David tried to cover their sin.

He called Bathsheba's husband, Uriah, back from the battlefield with an unsolicited furlough and sent him home. The next day David found out that Uriah had slept in the barracks with the other soldiers and the servants. "Dog the frog," he must have said. "Now I have to try something else."

The next evening David invited Uriah to his house for dinner and drinks. He figured some wine would take the edge off Uriah's conscience about sleeping at home in his bed while his comrades slept outdoors. This time, however, he gave him too much to drink.

It's said that when used as an aphrodisiac, liquor has a saturation point. It can help, but it can also hinder when too much is ingested. Actually, when liquor gives psychological arousal it's a depressant. Nevertheless, Uriah had more integrity drunk than David did sober. He staggered out of there and went to the barracks as he did the night before and went to sleep.

Then David was pressed to do something drastic. He wrote a note to Joab with instructions that said, "Set Uriah in the forefront of the hottest battle, and retreat from him, that he may be struck down and die." Ironically, he gave the note to Uriah to give to Joab. Uriah's innocent obedience forbade him from reading the note that was ordering his death.

David illustrates the nature of sin, which is to take us lower, and lower, and lower. David was at his lowest state ever. However, the story doesn't end there. His spiritual qualities come to the surface once again even from the low state he was in.

The "Fess Up"

Before the "*fess up*," David was festering up. He wrote in Psalm 38:7-8, "*There is no soundness in my flesh. I am feeble and severely broken.*" That is the result of unconfessed sins. The scenario of his confession is in 2 Samuel 12:13. There the prophet Nathan presented him a riddle about a man who hosted a traveler, but he did not prepare the man's meal from his own flock. He, instead, took his neighbor's only lamb. The "punch line" of the riddle was when Nathan asked the King what justice should be meted out to the man for his insensitivity, and David said he should repay his neighbor fourfold. Then Nathan replied, "*You are the man.*"

That's when David "*fessed up.*" His confession poured from his soul: "*And David said unto Nathan, 'I have sinned against the Lord.' And Nathan said unto David, 'The Lord has put away your sin. You shall not die.'*"

Any act of sin, regardless how small we may think it is, carries the penalty of death. We are supposed to die for any sin we commit. The Scripture says, "*The wages of sin is death.*" So every sin is punishable by death.

However, Nathan told David he wouldn't die because he had "*fessed up.*" This is when things began to turn around for David. His confession put the brakes on his downward slide of disobedience. And, not only did his confession put the brakes on his downward slide, it stopped that slide entirely. In fact, it not only stopped his downward slide, it reversed it.

David, as we all know, wrote various Psalms about his experiences, and Psalm 51 is the one he wrote about this situation. The entire psalm is his confession. It's shot through and through with contrition. The beginning of the psalm reads: "*Have mercy upon me, O God, according to Your loving kindness; according to the multitude of Your tender mercies. Blot out my transgressions. Wash me thoroughly from my iniquity, and cleanse me from my sin.*"

In the New Testament the clear teaching on forgiveness of sin is in 1 John 1:8-9. "*If we say we have no sin, we deceive ourselves and the truth is not in us. If we confess our sins, He is faithful and just to forgive us our sins and to cleanse us from all unrighteousness.*"

The most dialogue and questions in our new member classes are stimulated by *The Believer And Sin*. The most common question is: "Does this mean a Christian can do anything they want to do?" And, of course, the answer is "no." The confession isn't *permission to sin*; it's simply the *principle for forgiveness of sin*. Psalm 32:1 was also written out of this incident. It says, "*Blessed is he whose transgression is forgiven, whose sin is covered.*" When God forgives sin, He *covers* sin. But, that also means no one has the right to uncover a sin God has covered. Some Christians seem to enjoy revealing the sins of other Christians. It's said that the reason so many Christians are not witnesses is because we are all judges.

The Fix Up

After The *Foul Up* came The *Fess Up*, and then The *Fix Up*. The "*fess up*" permits God to *fix us up*. God will fix *us up* if we will "fess" up. And when God fixes it, it's completely fixed. The Bible says the blood of Jesus Christ, His Son, cleanses us from all our sin. His blood cleanses us, not water baptism. His blood cleanses us, not oil from a flask on your hand. His blood cleanses us, not when someone lays hands on us.

An old song asks, "What can wash away my sin?" And the answer given is, "Nothing, but the blood of Jesus." Another question is, "What can make me whole again?" And, it's the same answer, "Nothing, but the blood of Jesus."

David's problem, *after being forgiven by God*, came from people who wouldn't forgive him. Although the Bible says, "*He casts our sins in the sea of forgiveness and remembers them no more*," many people don't do that; they won't forgive us, or forget our sins. Some times people take it upon themselves to exact the punishment they feel we should have gotten from God. Wives refuse to restore their husbands, and husbands refuse to restore their wives. Children won't forgive their parents, and parents won't forgive their children.

That's what happened to David. Even though God had *fixed it up*, there was still *fallout* from the people. They rightfully held him to a higher standard, but they had also been recipients of God's forgiveness and mercy throughout their history.

A fellow named Ahithopel, who was David's counselor, used the occasion of David's sin to assist David's son, Absalom, in a rebellion against his father – an effort to take the kingdom. Absalom went to Hebron with a few followers and set himself up as king. However, 2 Samuel 15:11 indicates that the followers didn't know what was going on. It reads: "*And with Absalom went two hundred men from Jerusalem who were invited, and they went along innocently and did not know anything.*"

It was innocent ignorance on the part of these men. Nevertheless, David had to leave Jerusalem because of Absalom's rebellion, so he moved out with a group of loyal followers to go into hiding. In 2 Samuel 16:5 there is the story of a man named Shimei. While David was on his way out of the city head down, and shoulders drooped, Shimei came alongside and, walking stride for stride, cursed the King. However, he not only cursed David, he also threw rocks and dirt at him.

When people don't think you've gotten the punishment you deserve, they will try to do it for God.

One of David's soldiers volunteered to take care of him, but David forbade him. Another soldier asked permission to *take him down*, since he wouldn't let the other soldier *take him out*. But, again, David refused to let them touch Shimei.

That's yet another time when his Godly character came to the surface. The incident proves, however, that the *Fix Up* does not always do away with the *Fallout*.

The Finish Up

Absalom's rebellion was eventually put down. King David was returned to Jerusalem and was restored to his throne. His return to Jerusalem was the reverse of retreat from Jerusalem, including the reappearance of Shemei. This time Shemei came alongside when David returned to Jerusalem as he did when David was going out. However, this time he wasn't content to walk stride for stride at a distance. This time he approached David, bowing as he came, and he wasn't cussing or throwing rocks and dirt. This time he is saying, "*Oh King, live forever. You're the best king we ever had.*" This should teach us to be careful about writing people off before God does. We should be careful about putting somebody down who God may want to raise back up again. No one has the right to count somebody out who God wants to use again.

God restored David.

And despite his sins, he finished the task God assigned to him. He went on to become the greatest king of all the kings of Israel.

Don't let anyone try to push you out of Christian service. Don't let anyone try to shame you out of serving the Lord because you stumbled and fell. No one has the right to do that. So, if you fall, "*fess up*," be forgiven and then finish.

Abraham still became the father of the faithful *after* he had fallen. Moses was eulogized by God after he had fallen. God didn't allow any pallbearers to carry his body or gravediggers to dig the hole. He did it Himself, and stood there at the foot of Moses' grave and said, "*There shall never be another prophet likened unto Moses who knew God face to face.*" And Moses received that eulogy after he had fallen.

Old cussing and cutting Peter went on to become the chief apostle after he had fallen. The list is endless. Other men and women were restored to service after they had fallen.

This is a story for fallen people. This isn't for someone who has made his or her own halo. This isn't a story for a person who can see only the wrong in someone else, and can never see it in him or herself.

This is a story for fallen people. It's a good story for someone who is strong at times, and weak at other times. This is a story for someone who stumbles and even falls down sometimes.

You need to know that you can still finish. You can still be the man God can use in His service. You can still be the woman that God needs for a witness in these critical times. It doesn't matter how low you may have sunk. The God I serve sits high, but He can reach low. You can't fall beyond the reach of His hand, or beyond the orbit of His grace.

You can still finish no matter what has transpired in your life. The grace of God can meet you in your weakest area. The grace of God can meet you at the most shameful area of your life. God can help you to finish. Through this shameful experience, David was still *a man after God's own heart.*

THE KING IS DEAD: LONG LIVE THE KING!

Chapter Twenty-Two

1 Kings 1:1-4, 2:10-12; 1 Chronicles 29:26-30

"*For David, after he had served his own generation by the will of God, fell asleep was buried with his fathers, and saw corruption.*" Not even King David was exempt from his mortality. As a matter of fact, he personally announced the imminent end of his life from his deathbed with these words: "*I go the way of the ends of all the earth.*"

For many Christians, David is the choice favorite of all the Old Testament saints. He is one both to *love* and *learn* from. His life not only *refreshes* us, it *represents* us.

I have visited the gravesites of many saints in Israel, but none, other than the Empty Tomb, gave me the emotional experience I had at David's tomb. He touches us in a personal, peculiar way. He *warms* us and *warns* us with his life. From his ancient past, David warns us against yielding to temptation. His fleshly fallibility drives home the stern words of the Apostle Paul: "*Let him who thinks he stands take heed, lest he fall.*"

Although David was beset with *frailties* and *flaws*, he still managed to have an *ever-ascending life.* Without a doubt, he made his share of bad decisions and wrong choices, true enough. He sinned grievously, but overall, considering the sum total of his life, he still managed to always be on an upward trek in his spiritual maturity. He was always ascending to reach for new levels of commitment unto God. He was always progressing toward more greatness. He was not a mediocre, status quo, stuck-in-the-mud kind of person. This is evidenced by his personal and professional life.

It was under the reign of David that Israel became a worshipping people again. He had the inspiration to restore the Ark of the Covenant, the piece of furniture that was central to their worship. The Ark had been out of the presence of God's people for nearly fifty years.

He structured the order of the priests into twenty-four courses. He organized the temple singers into a mass two hundred eighty-eight voice-choir. The construction of the temple was his vision, and even though he was denied the privilege of building it, he still picked the site and provided most of the material for the construction.

He led in giving, offerings to finance the construction of the temple. And he led in urging others to give. Serving God was the foremost priority on his agenda. He epitomized the words of our Lord, "*Seek ye first the kingdom of God and all these things will be added unto you.*"

However, in the words of the poet, "*Death thunders at the palace gates of the king and at the dwelling of the poor. There is no escape.*" So on one fateful day the dreaded announcement was made, "The King is dead," and he was laid to rest with those who sleep within the tomb.

The Appointed Life

For the most part, David lived in harmony with God, and that's the best compliment that can be given to any child of God. Many Christians don't do that *seriously* or *successfully*. Unfortunately, we can miss the best blessings by not living in harmony with God.

God had specific blessings appointed for David, and He has blessings appointed for you and me. No one can stop or block the blessings that God intends to appoint in your life.

David was appointed to the throne of Israel. This shows us how far God can work above our expectations and imaginations. It wasn't on David's mind to become king. He didn't finagle or pull any shenanigans to become king. God Sovereignly appointed him King of Israel, but please note that it all started for David out of his close relationship with God. David was close to God during his boyhood days. He was a teenager when he was chosen and anointed to be king. It's always noteworthy when a person's relationship with God can be traced back to his or her childhood. It's a strong testimony to become acquainted with God as a girl or a boy and to never lose that contact.

Psalm 23, known as the "Nightingale of the Psalms," is perhaps the most beloved of all one hundred fifty of them. Most Christians know it from memory. But, David did not write Psalm 23 in his senior years. The lyrics of Psalm 23 are a composition of David when he was a teenager. His close relationship with God was cemented when he was a shepherd boy during those long lazy days and long cold nights beneath the twinkling stars. God appointed his life. God gave him *abilities* and *advancements*, as well as *promotions* and *protection*.

Nevertheless, "God is not a respecter of persons." God has appointments on reserve for whoever will walk humbly beneath the shadow of His grace. God wants to bless us and lift us up and make us examples of His greatness. God is always looking for someone whom He can bless. He is looking for someone who can handle the kinds of blessings He can deliver.

God can "pile 'em on" if we could act right *after* He "piles 'em on." David is proof. It's a long stretch from being a shepherd to becoming a sovereign over a nation. An *appointed life* is a blessed life.

The Appropriated Life

In Psalm 27 David says, "*The Lord is my life and my salvation. Whom shall I fear*?" The interpretation of those words is a reflection on God's appropriated blessings in David's life. The conclusion is that the God who provides *salvation* also provides *safety*.

In another psalm he wrote, "*In the time of trouble, He shall hide me in His pavilion*." It's inconsistent to trust God in spiritual matters and not trust him in temporal matters. We are often guilty of not trusting God completely. However, God can appropriate whatever blessings we need. He is not a one-dimensional God.

David's life challenges us today to deepen the capacity of our relationship with God. The deeper our capacity, the greater God can use us and bless us. With that deeper capacity, we will be available for whatever blessings God has for us.

Notwithstanding, "*whatever*" also includes what God does *not* desire for us. A blessed life is not only when God *presents blessings*, a blessed life is when He also *prevents blessings*. There are some blessings we need God to prevent from coming to us. Maturity as a Christian means we can thank God for some blessings we *didn't* receive.

I'm truly grateful for the doors God has opened for me. But, my goodness, I'm absolutely truly grateful for the doors He closed for me. A blessed life is not only when God plants into your life, but also when God plucks up out of your life. A blessed life is not only when God is sowing into your life, a blessed life is also when God is snatching out of your life.

Without a doubt, David had an appropriated life, and so can we. When you have an appropriated life, it doesn't matter who your enemies are, or what they may be saying or doing behind your back. It doesn't matter what obstacles you may face. Nothing, or no one, can stop your forward progress when God has blessed you with an *appropriated life*.

The Approved Life

The fact that David had an *approved life* can be gleaned from inscription that described him as "*a man after God's own heart.*" It really doesn't matter who *disapproves* of you when God *approves* you. It doesn't matter who *puts you down* when God has determined *to lift you up*. It doesn't matter who thinks there's *nothing to you* when God says He intends to make something out of you.

David had an *approved life*. No one can deny that the Lord was in David's life. For the person who may raise the question, "How could God stamp His divine approval over David's checkered life?" The answer is by the *application* of His grace and the *appropriation* of *His mercy*. After all, that's the same way He approves your life and mine.

The Apostle Paul theologized what it means for God to approve a life. He made up a word and he called it "justification." Justification is when God *erases our sin*, and *eradicates our sin*, and *expunges* our sin.

If you think that's something, that's not all. Then God treats us as if we had *never* sinned.

And if you think *that's* something, then God bestows on us His righteousness. That's what it means to have an *approved life*.

David's inspired words address the matter in Psalm 16. And Peter quoted from Psalm 16 in Acts 2: 25. David spoke in what I call "*a justified tense*." You see, in regular grammatical terms there is the *present, past,* and *future tenses*. However, God talks in a *justified tense*.

Here are the words from Acts 2:25, "*And David spoke concerning Him: 'I foresaw the Lord always before my face. He is on my right hand that I should not be moved.'*" The key word is "*always*." How could David say he always kept the Lord before his face? He wasn't looking at the Lord when he saw Bathsheba bathing that night. This is an example of when the Bible speaks in a *jus-*

tified tense. It was spoken after the *application of grace* and the *appropriation of mercy* for his sins.

If there was any sin that could seemingly disqualify David from having an *approved life*, it would be his adulterous affair with Bathsheba; that is, by human estimation. However, from God's perspective, it's a different story. When God speaks about sins in His Word, it's as if He has a sign hanging over the sin, one that says "*before*" and another sign that says "*after*." As we remember what David did to *cause* the sin, we also have to remember what David did to *correct* the sin, which is why God can speak of David's sins and our sins in a *justified tense*.

Another scripture says, "*David walked uprightly and kept all the laws of God*." What? That's God talking in His *justified tense*. That's after the sin has been erased, eradicated and expunged. However, continuing on to verse 26 of Acts 2 are these words: "*Therefore my heart rejoiced and my tongue was glad; moreover, my flesh shall rest in hope*."

Why was David so confident about resting in hope at his death? Verse 27 has the clue: "*For You will not leave my soul in Hades (Sheol). Nor will You allow Your Holy One to see corruption*." This was a prophetical reference by David. David was also a prophet, and he had insight about the resurrection of Messiah.

Most Old Testament saints didn't even see the Messiah dying, not to mention His resurrection. David saw the Lord's resurrection, which is why he could say, "*My flesh shall rest in hope*." Another reference to his hope of resurrection is in Psalm 17:15, which reads: "*I shall be satisfied when I wake in His likeness*." Paul expressed it this way: "*That I may know Him and the power of His resurrection.*" The proof of David's *approved life was his assurance of his resurrection*.

The sickroom and the deathbed in the king's palace was the scene of the end of an era. No king has ever "kinged" like David. He was **The King of Israel** "*first and last*." Nevertheless, the king was *in declining health* and *in death's hands*. But, even though he was *in declining health* and *in death's hands*, he had a *definite hope*.

He said, "*My flesh shall rest in hope.*"

Ultimately, the dreaded announcement had to be circulated throughout the kingdom. From tribe to tribe, the runners came with the message that the King is dead. The fact is that great lives don't end at the grave. We live on in people's memories when God has approved our lives.

In my earlier years, the announcement that "The King is dead," followed by the statement, "Long live the King," seemed contradictory. However, the meaning is clear now. The memories of a person live on in the hearts of other people. Each time Psalm 23 is read, or recited, it's an acknowledgment that David still lives. Every time a choir sings the anthem, "Lift up your head, Oh ye gates, and be ye lifted up ye everlasting doors, and the King of Glory shall come in," it's an acknowledgment that David still lives.

When the people of God are ministered to by the comforting words in Psalm 46, "*God is my refuge and my strength, a very present help in the time of trouble,*" it's an indication that David still lives.

On his deathbed, he uttered these words, "*I am going the way of all the men of the earth.*" When he was near to death he said, "*My flesh shall rest in hope.*" In anticipation and in hope of the resurrection he declared, "*I will be satisfied when I wake in His likeness.*"

Like King David, Christians need a testimony about their dying hour. Of all the testimonies we may have about the goodness of God, and how God has brought us and kept us, we still need another testimony. We need a testimony about our dying hour.

I realize the topic of dying is not one readily discussed by many people, including many Christians. People like to celebrate birthdays, but won't concentrate on their "death day." A lot is revealed about how a person lived by the way he or she faces their mortality. Someone said, "As you live, so shall you die." If you live close to God, you can die close to God. If you live in harmony with God, you can die in harmony with God. Every child of God needs a testimony about his or her dying hour.

The old saints made it a part of their prayers saying, "Let my last days be my best days. In my dying hour, I want to lay my head on Jesus' breast and breathe my life sweetly away. And, when I come down to the Jordan, meet me there and cross me over on a calm tide."

My testimony is from the song that goes like this: "If I don't wake up in the morning, everything will be all right." I have another one as a backup: "Let the fiery, clouded pillar lead me on my journey home. When I tread the verge of Jordan, bid my anxious fears subside. Bear me through the swirling currents and land me safe on Canaan's side." And, I have another: "It is well with my soul."

Even in his dying hour, David's spiritual quality rose to the surface. His final words underscored his faith in God and his hope of eternal life. "*Now the days of David drew near that he should die, and he charged Solomon his son, saying, 'I go the way of all the earth; be strong, therefore, and prove your self a man*'" (2 Kings 2:1-2).

"*So he died in a good old age, full of days and riches and honor; and Solomon his son reigned in his place*" (1 Chronicles 29:28).

David lives on in the hearts of many Christians as their favorite Old Testament Bible character. *The King is dead; long live the King.*